Check out
Global Doodle Gems
Easter Collection Volume 1

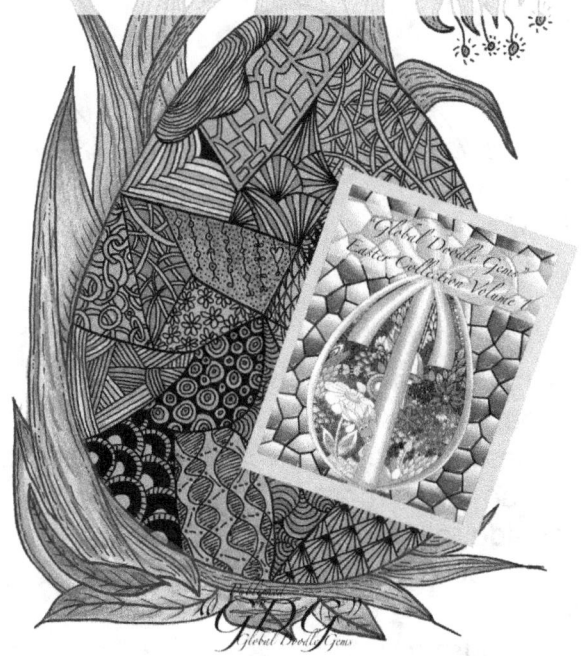

Global Doodle Gems
Easter Collection
Volume 2

CoverArt

by

Rover Hsiao

&

Inge Boogaers

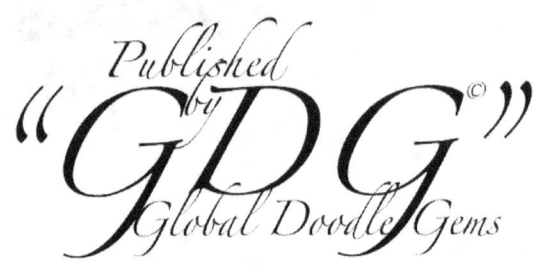

Share your colored versions with us ! We love seeing your results and hearing from you we are social !

The Official FB book page, stay on top of what we have in the works !
www.facebook.com/globaldoodlegems
The Community group, share your colored pages, meet the artists, enjoy exclusive freebies, take part in community Charity books and so much more......
www.facebook.com/groups/globaldoodlegems/
Follow us on Twitter.... @GlobalDoodlegem
We are on Instagram too
@globaldoodlegems for instagram
...and if you are not social like that we have a blog
globaldoodlegems.wordpress.com

Copyright © 2017 Global Doodle Gems
All rights are reserved by Global Doodle Gems.
Duplication of pages for personal use are allowed. You are invited to color the pages then scan/post your coloured versions to social networks, mentioning the book title and author/artist (Global Doodle Gems).
All artwork and images are protected by copyright laws. This book or any portion thereof may not, otherwise, be reproduced and/or distributed or transmitted without the express written permission of the artist/publisher of Global Doodle Gems.
All of us from the Global Doodle Gems wish you a colortastic time and look forward to seeing your wonderful color results online !

Contributing Artists

Alfred E Villanueva
Carol Mayer
LynniEx Doodles
Johanna Ans
Jenny Wei
Audrey Sagh
Arianne Schimmel
Tammy Stansbery
Inge Boogaers
Pica Wu
Rover Hsiao

Contributing Artist
Alfred E. Villanueva
Philippines
Facebook : viworksart2015

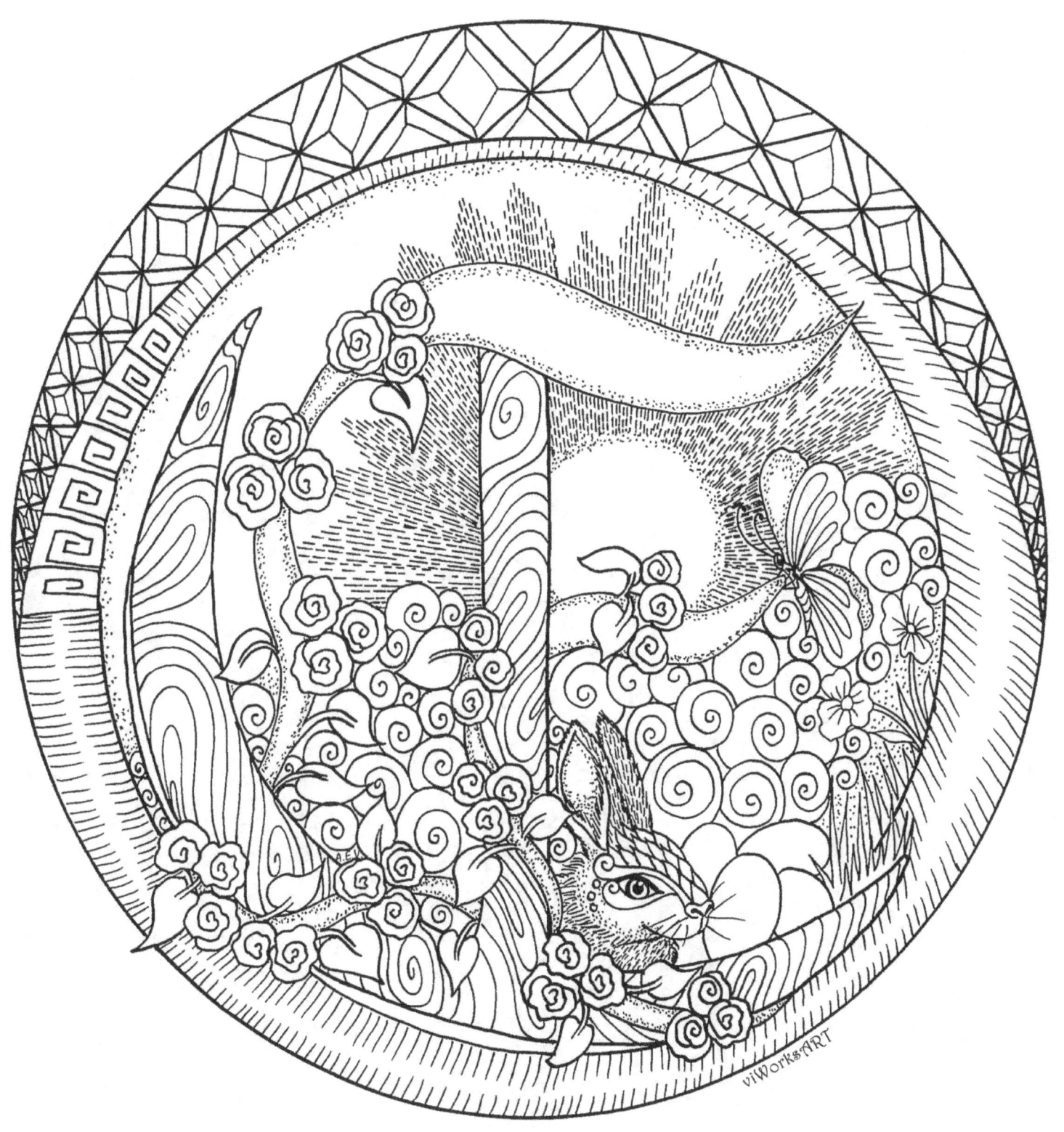

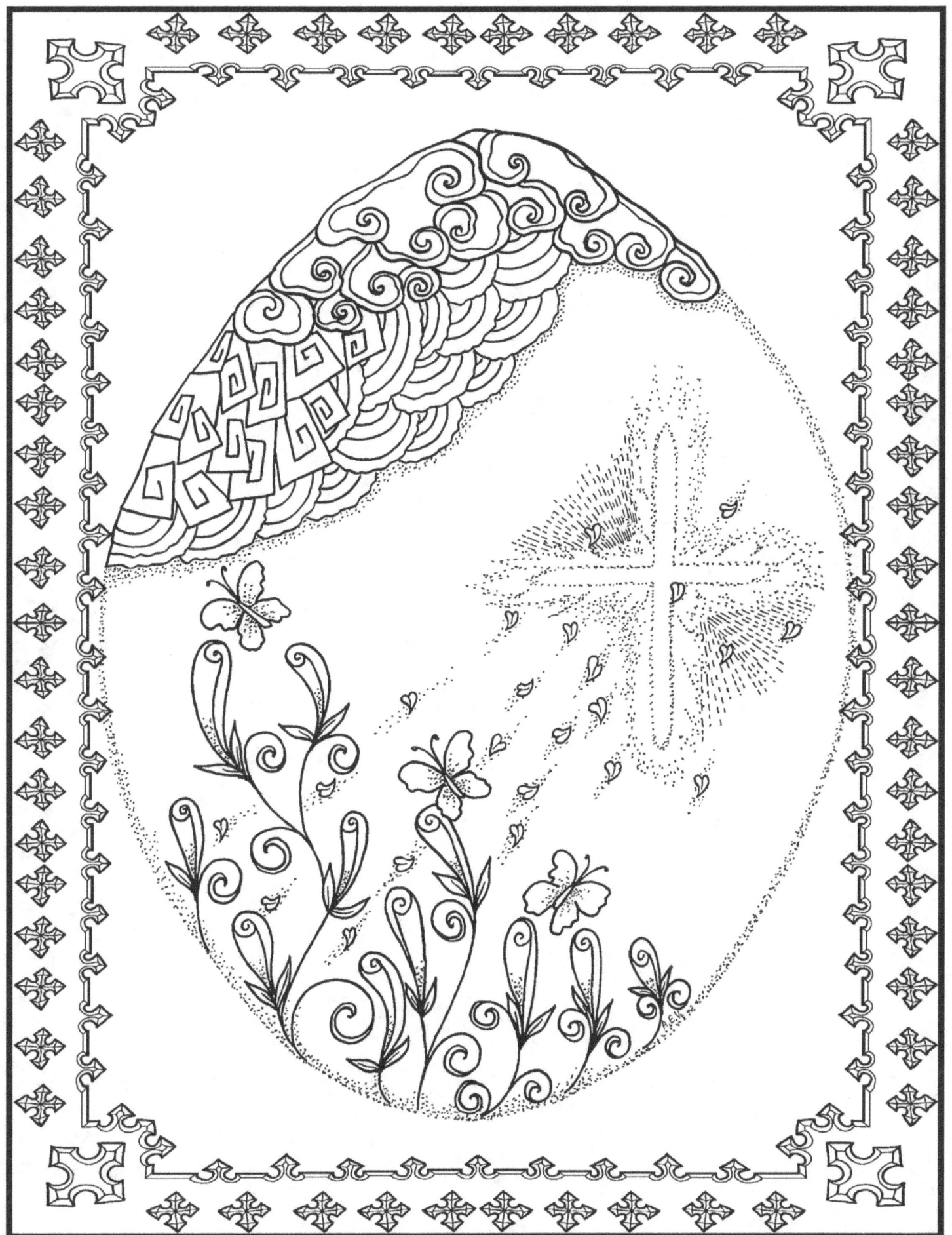

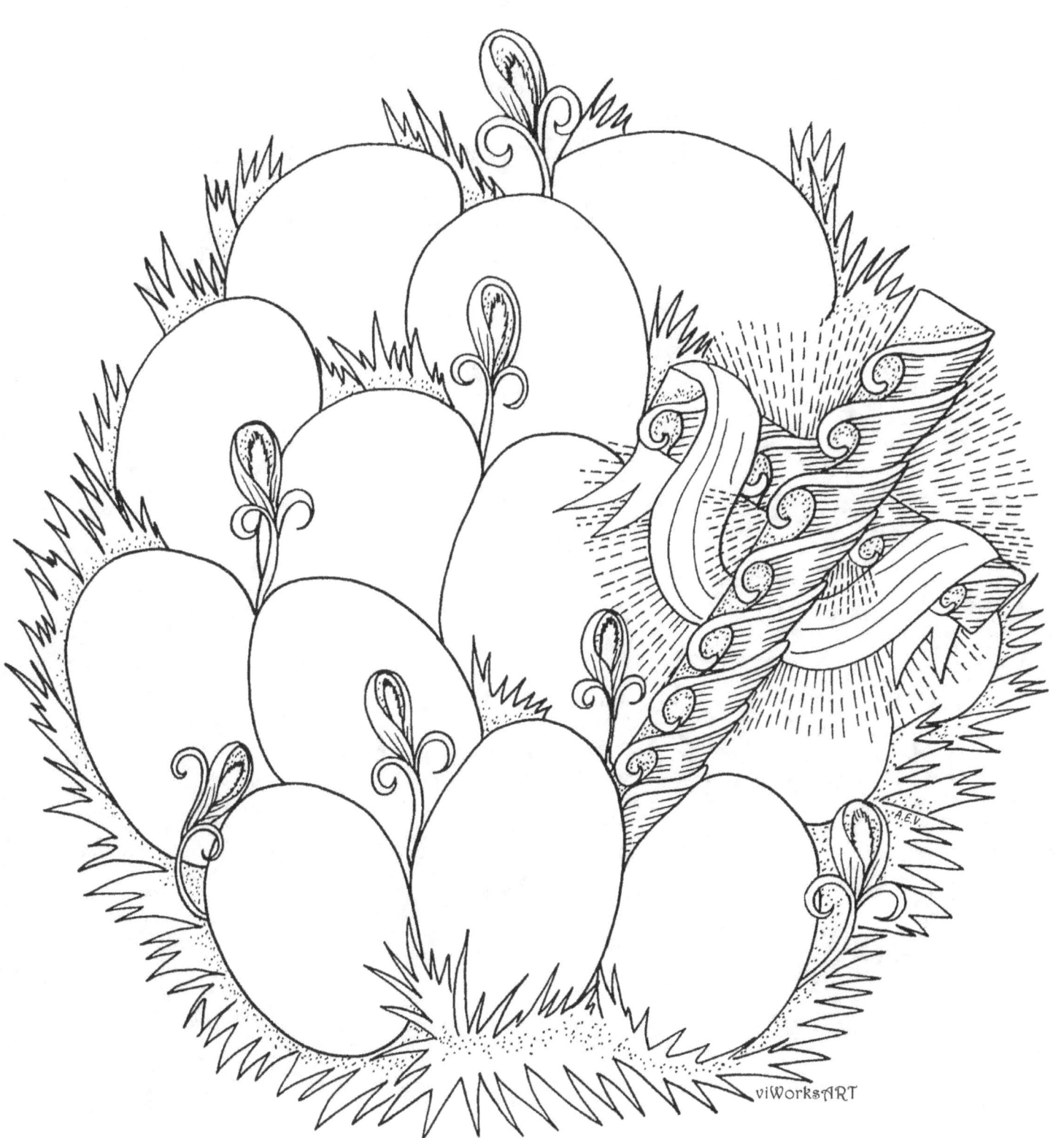

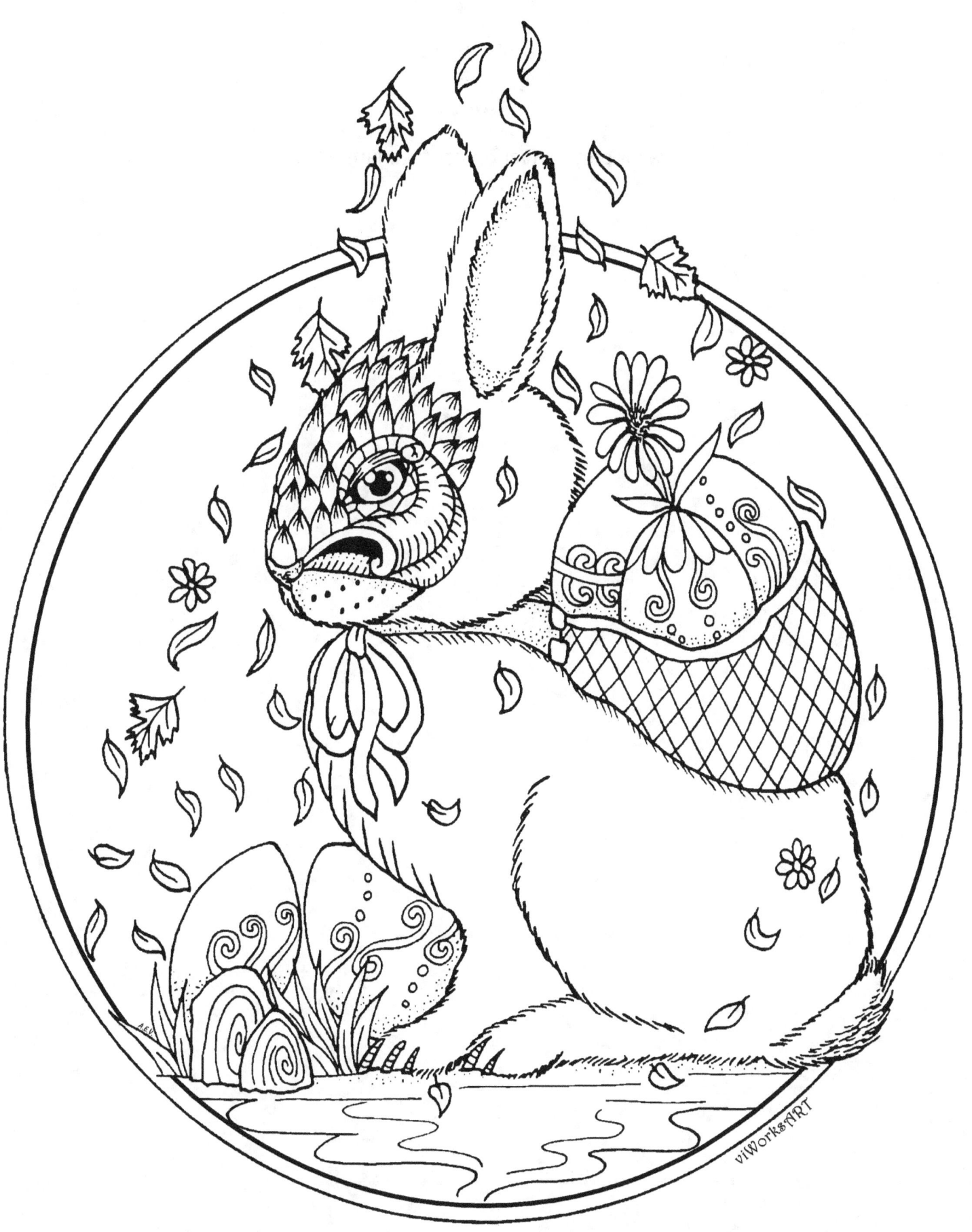

Contributing Artist
Carol Mayer
Canada

www.etsy.com/shop/canadianartbeat

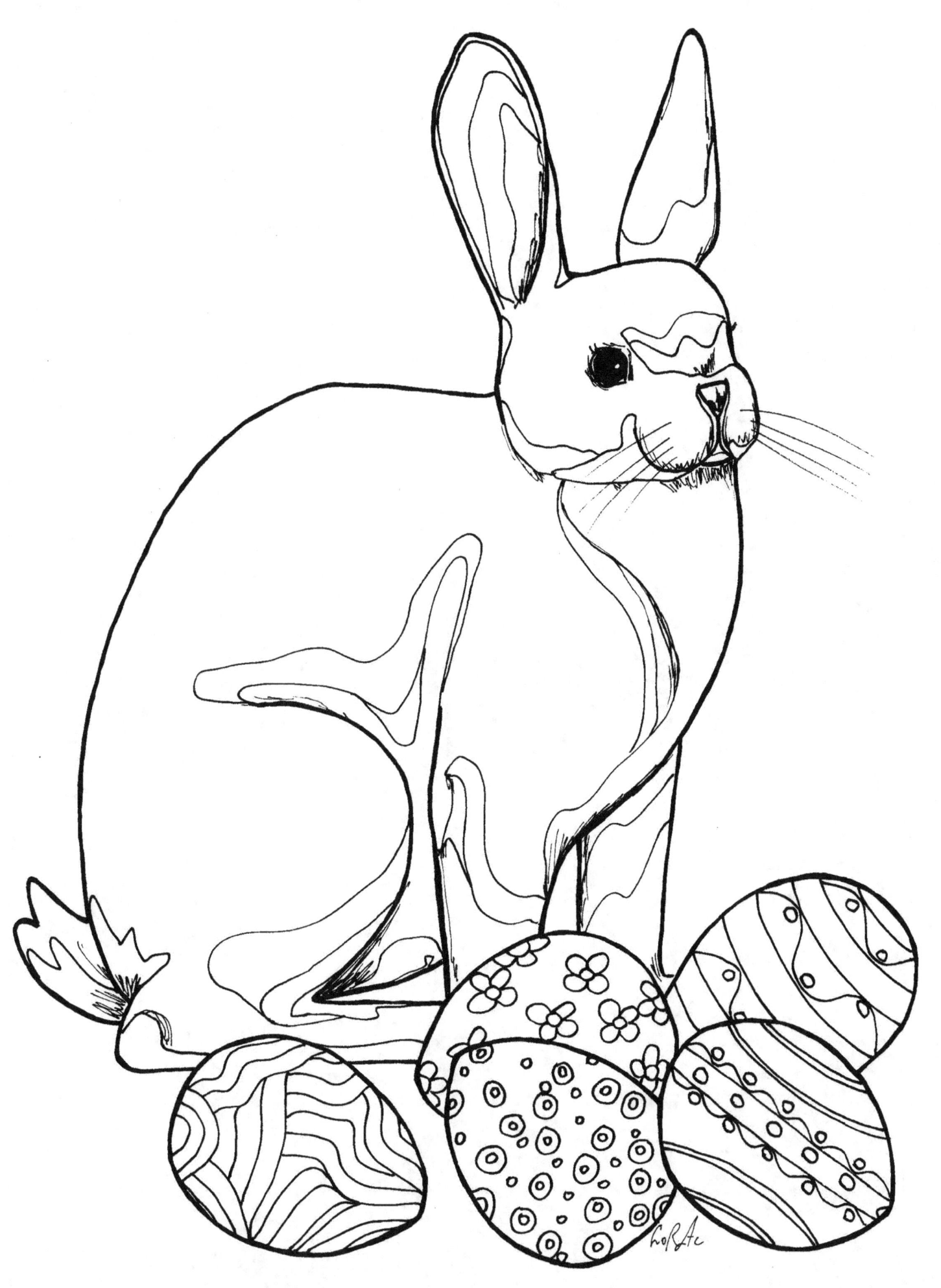

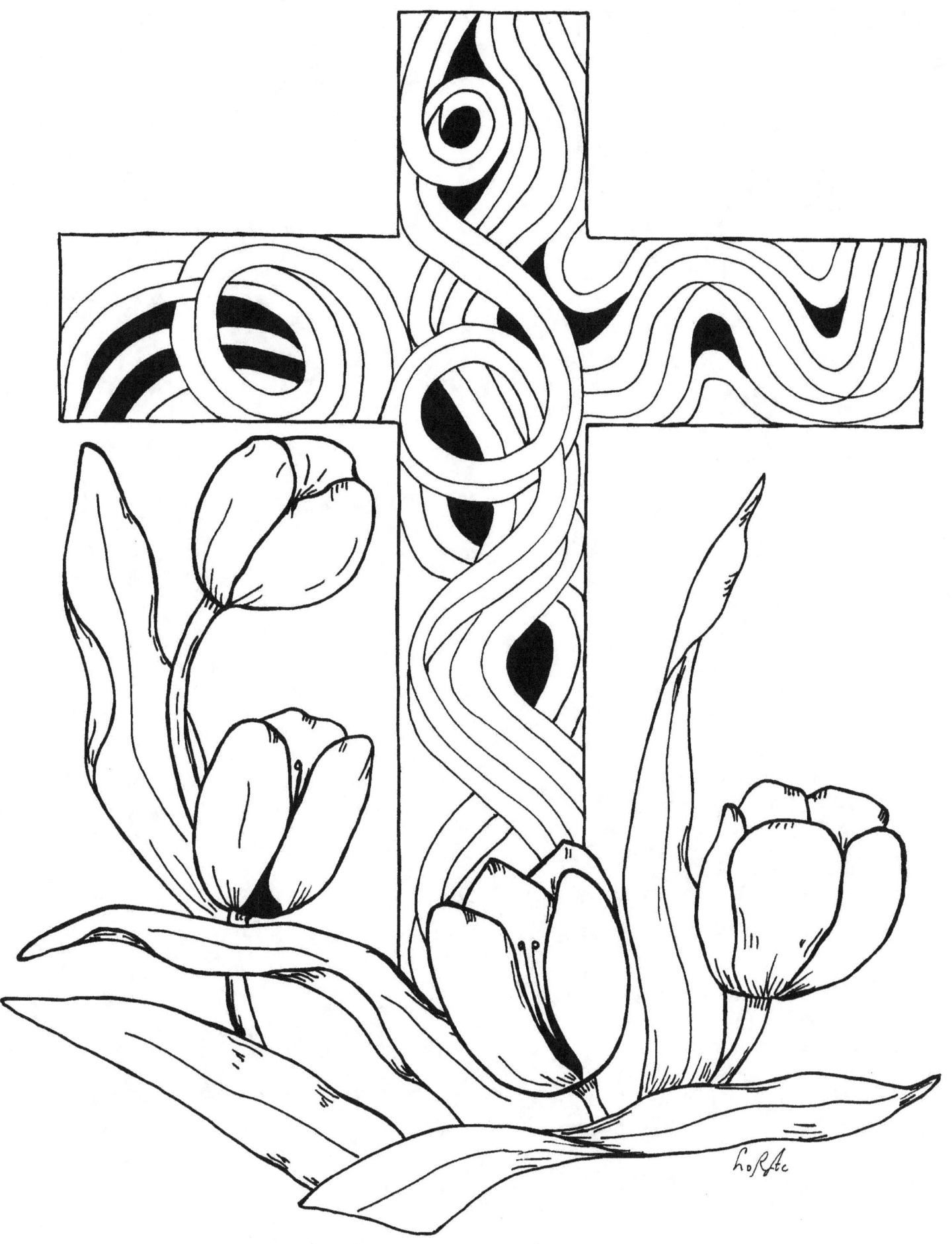

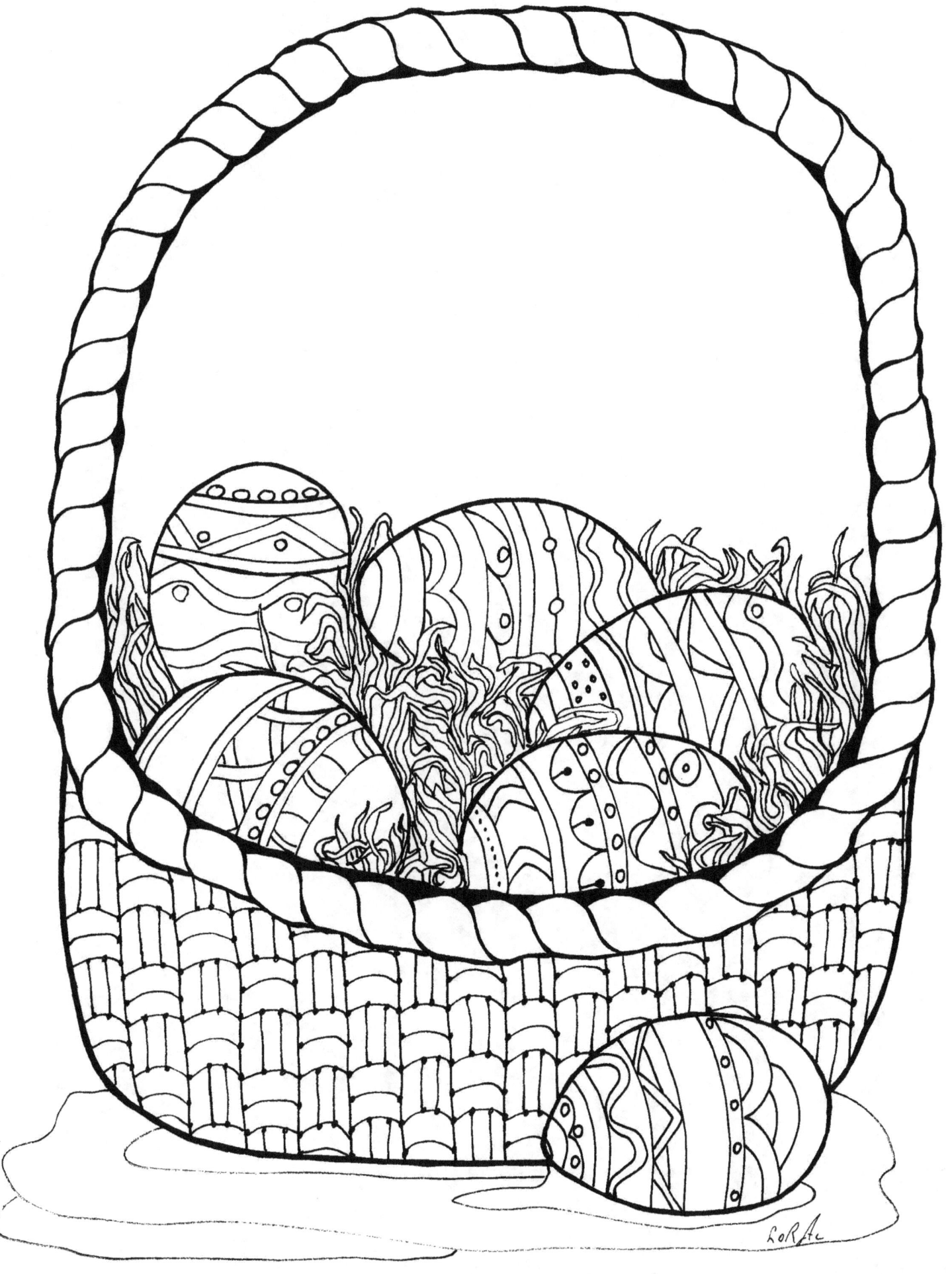

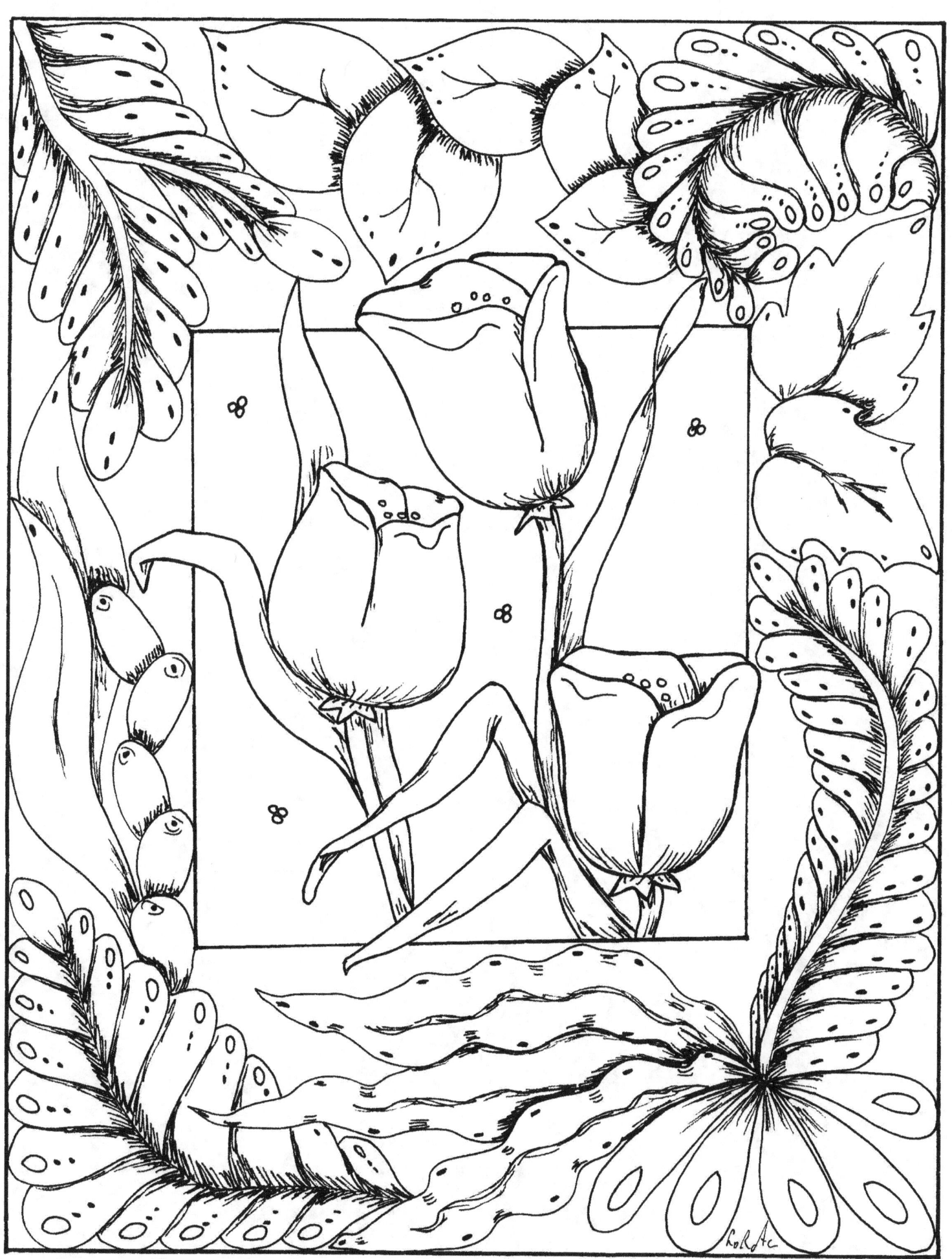

Contributing Artist
Lynniex Doodles
England

Facebook : Lynniex Doodles

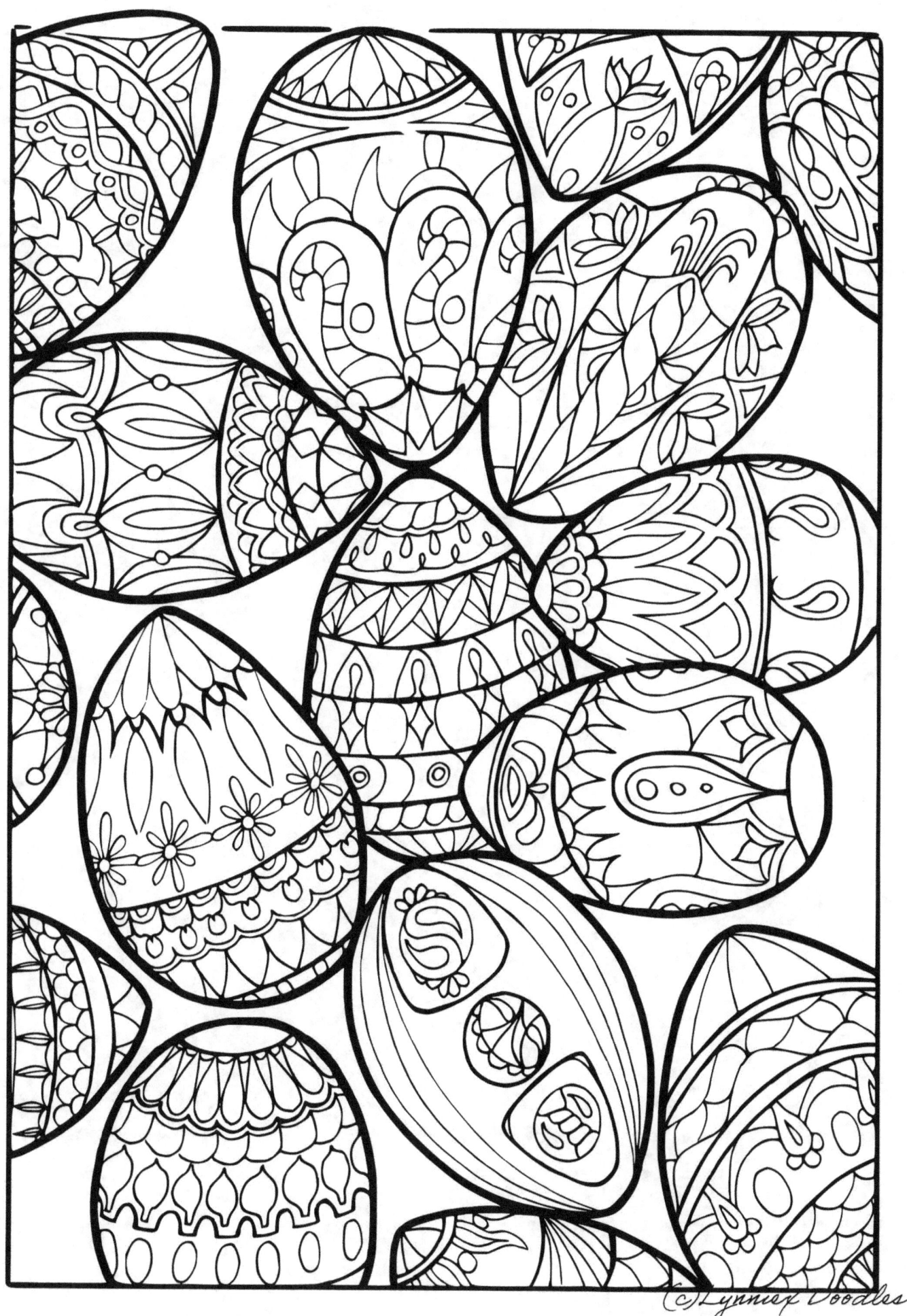

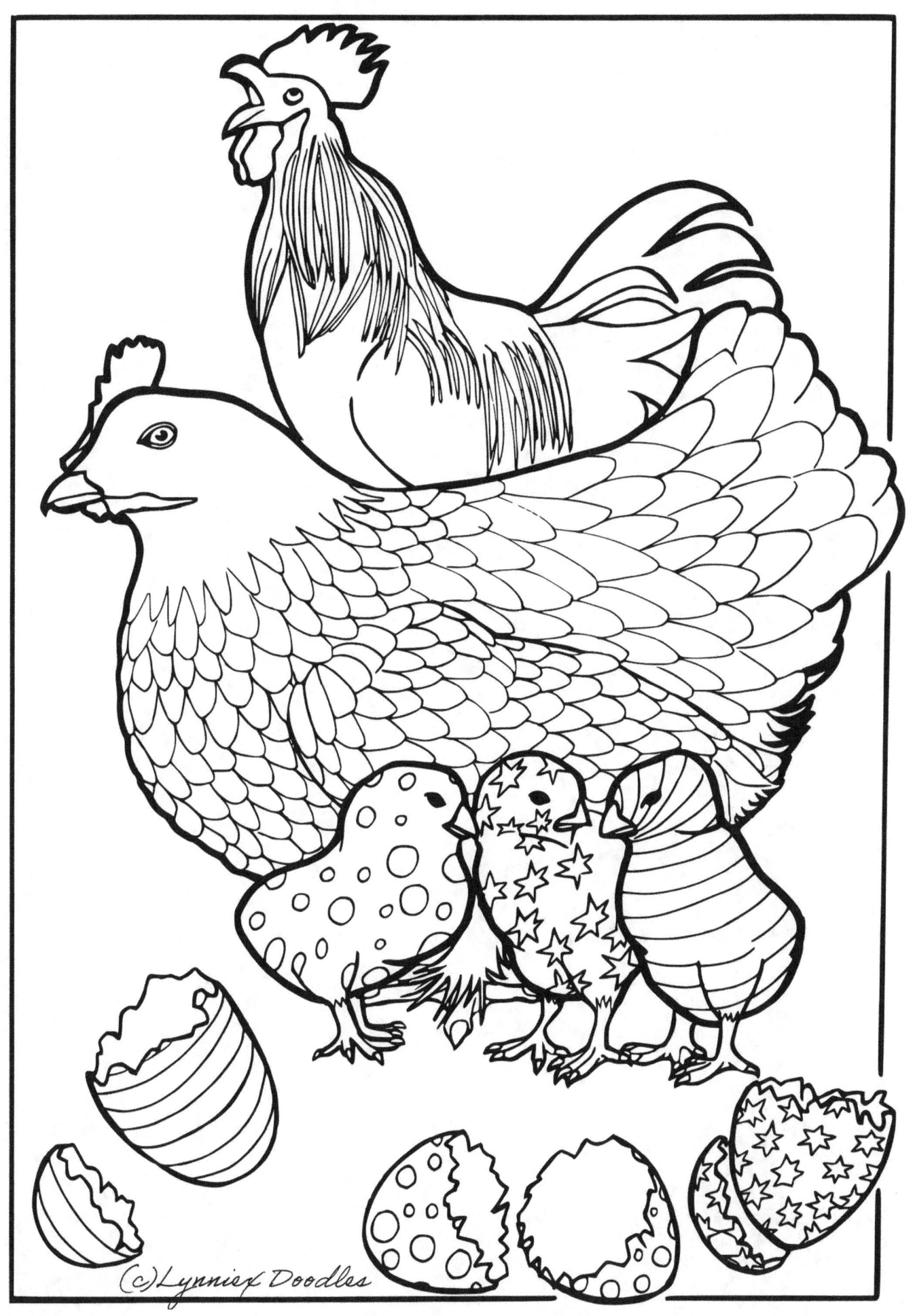

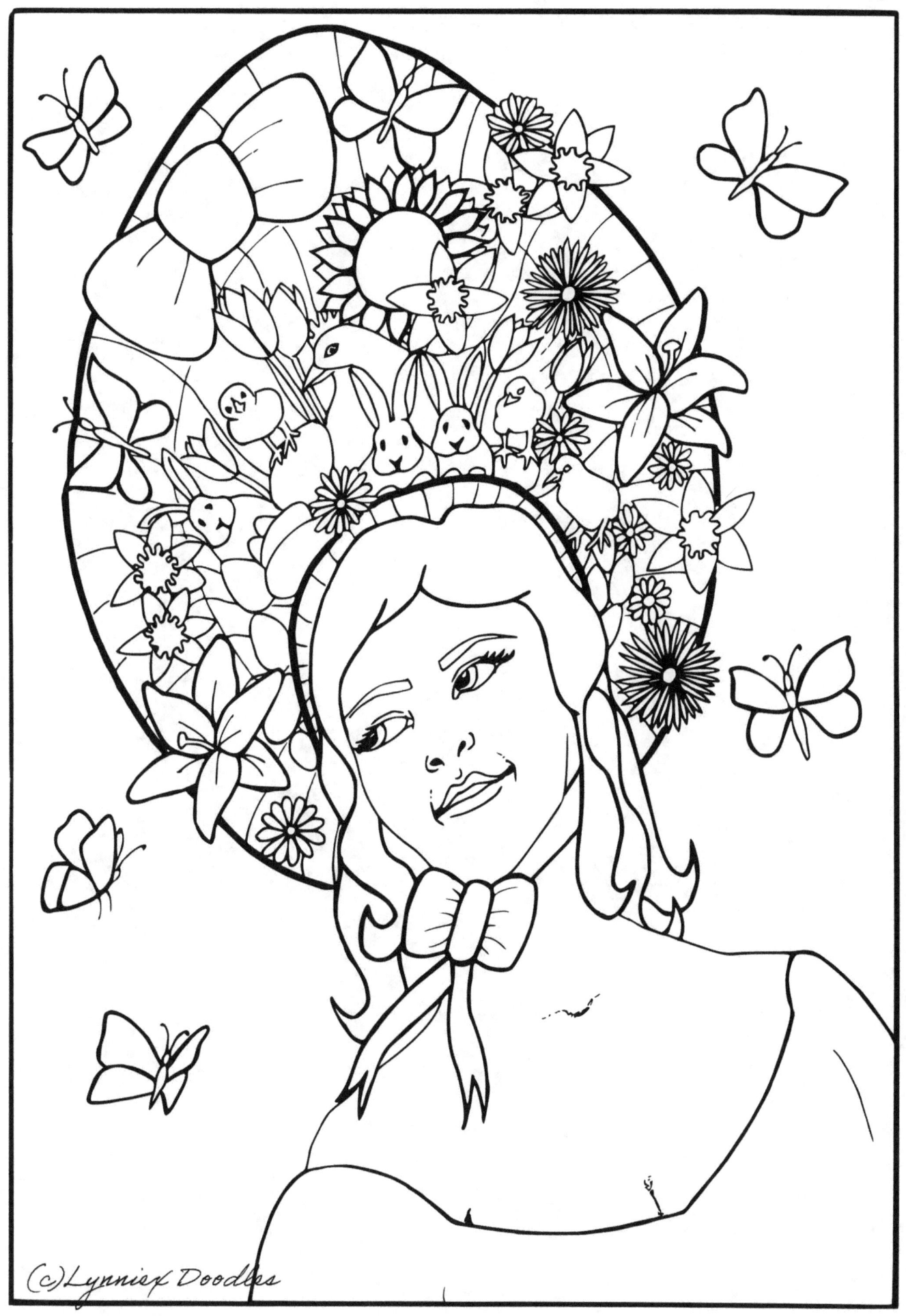

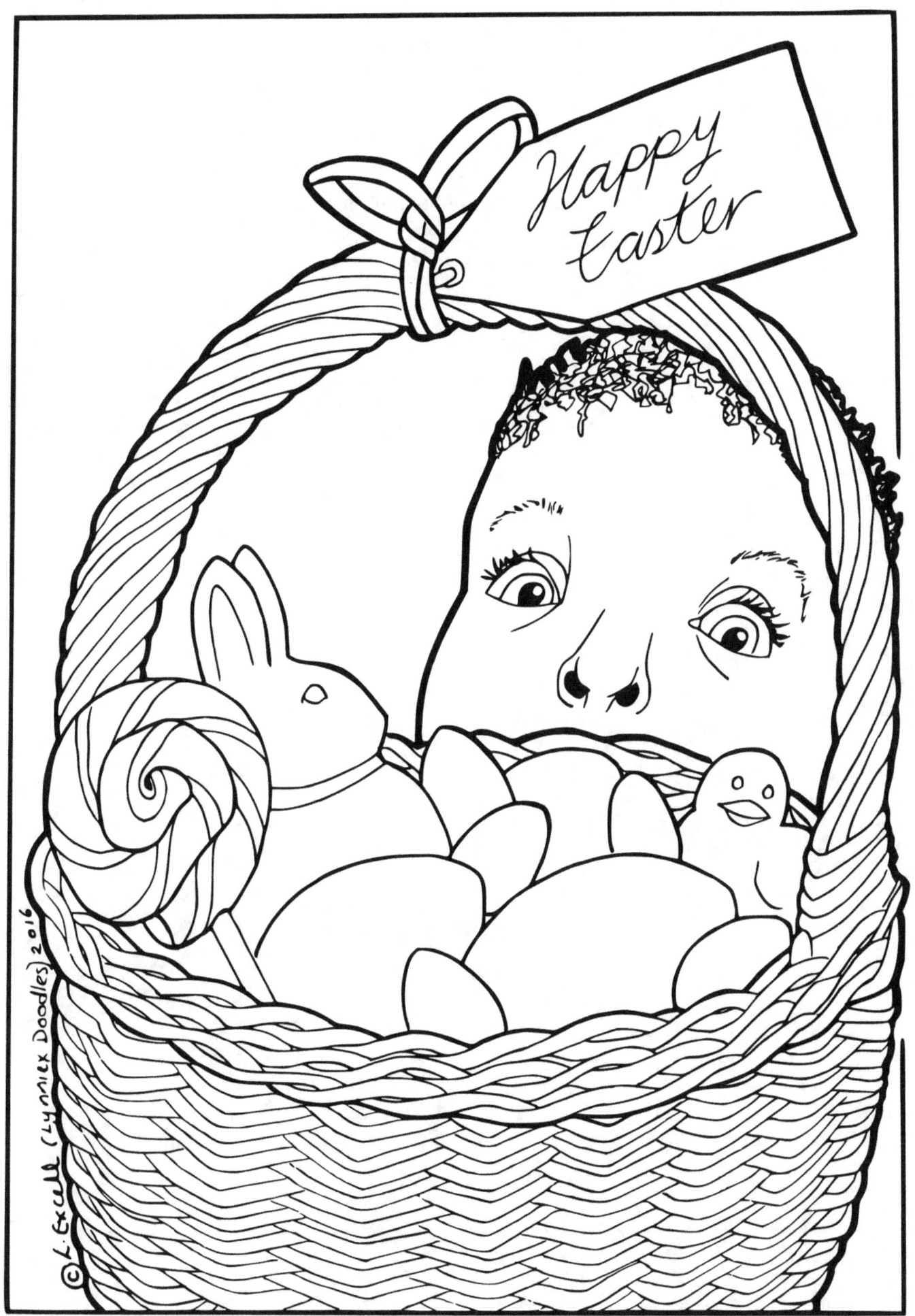

Contributing Artist
Johanna Ans
The Netherlands

Facebook : JohannaAns

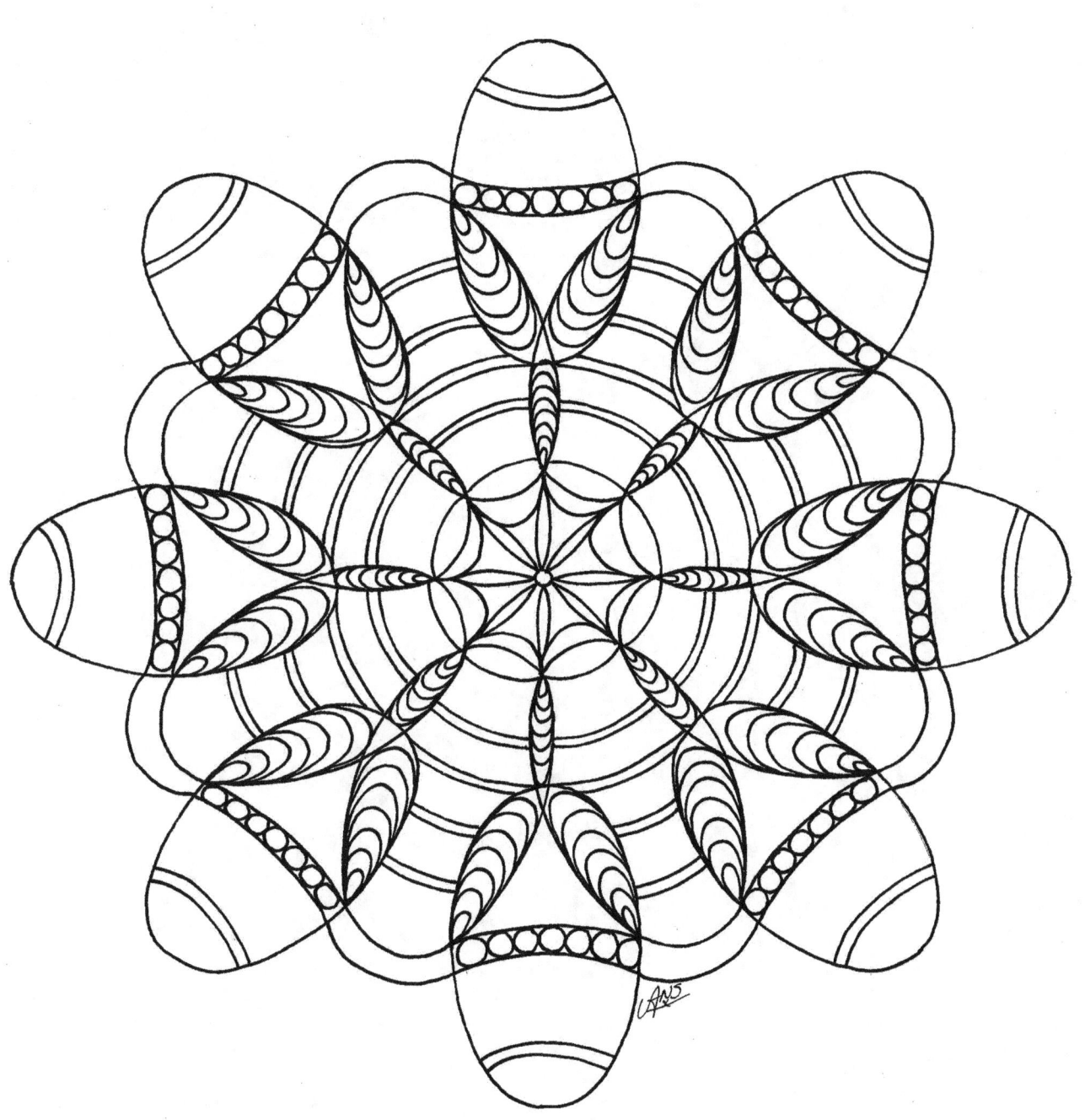

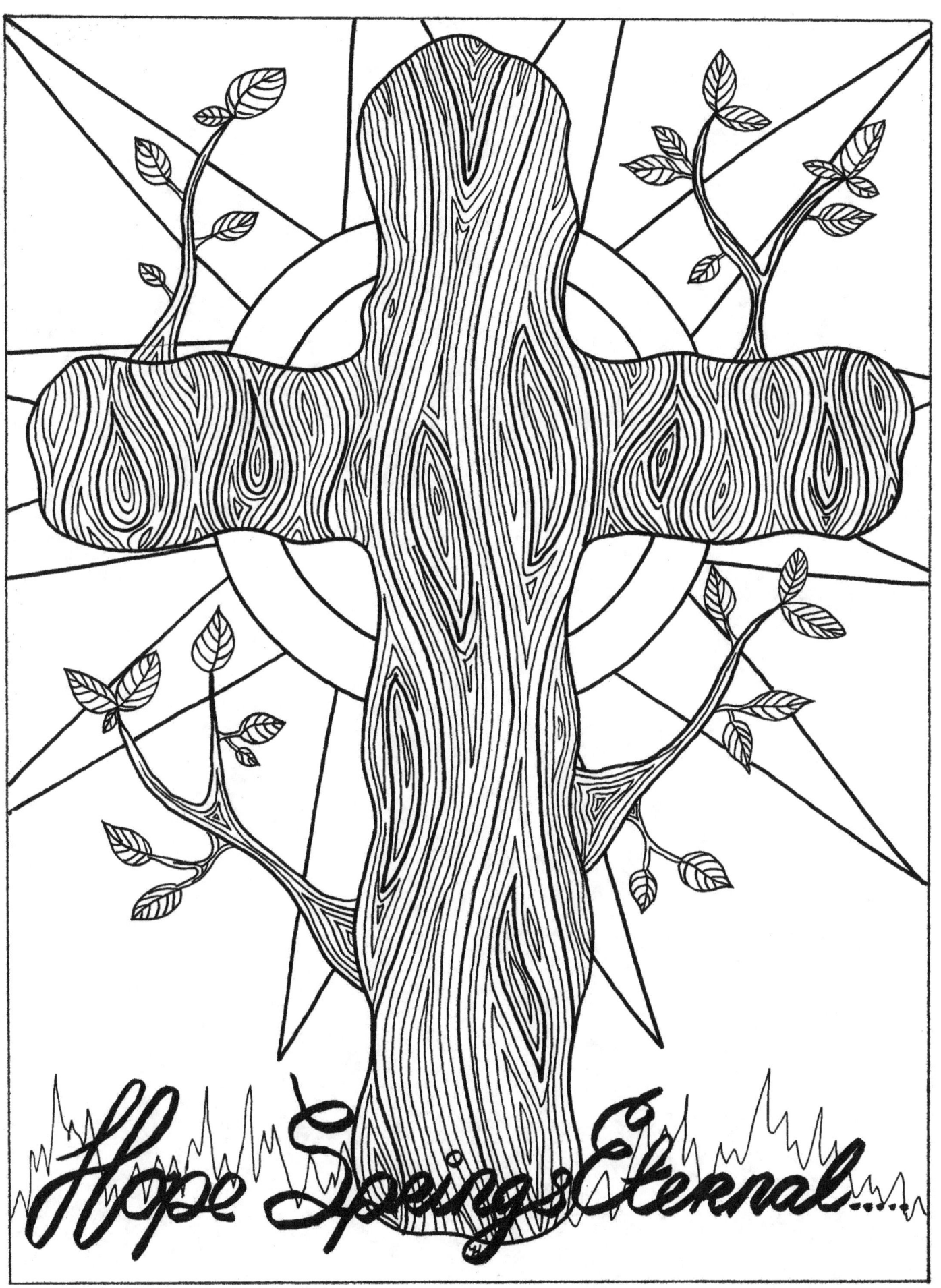

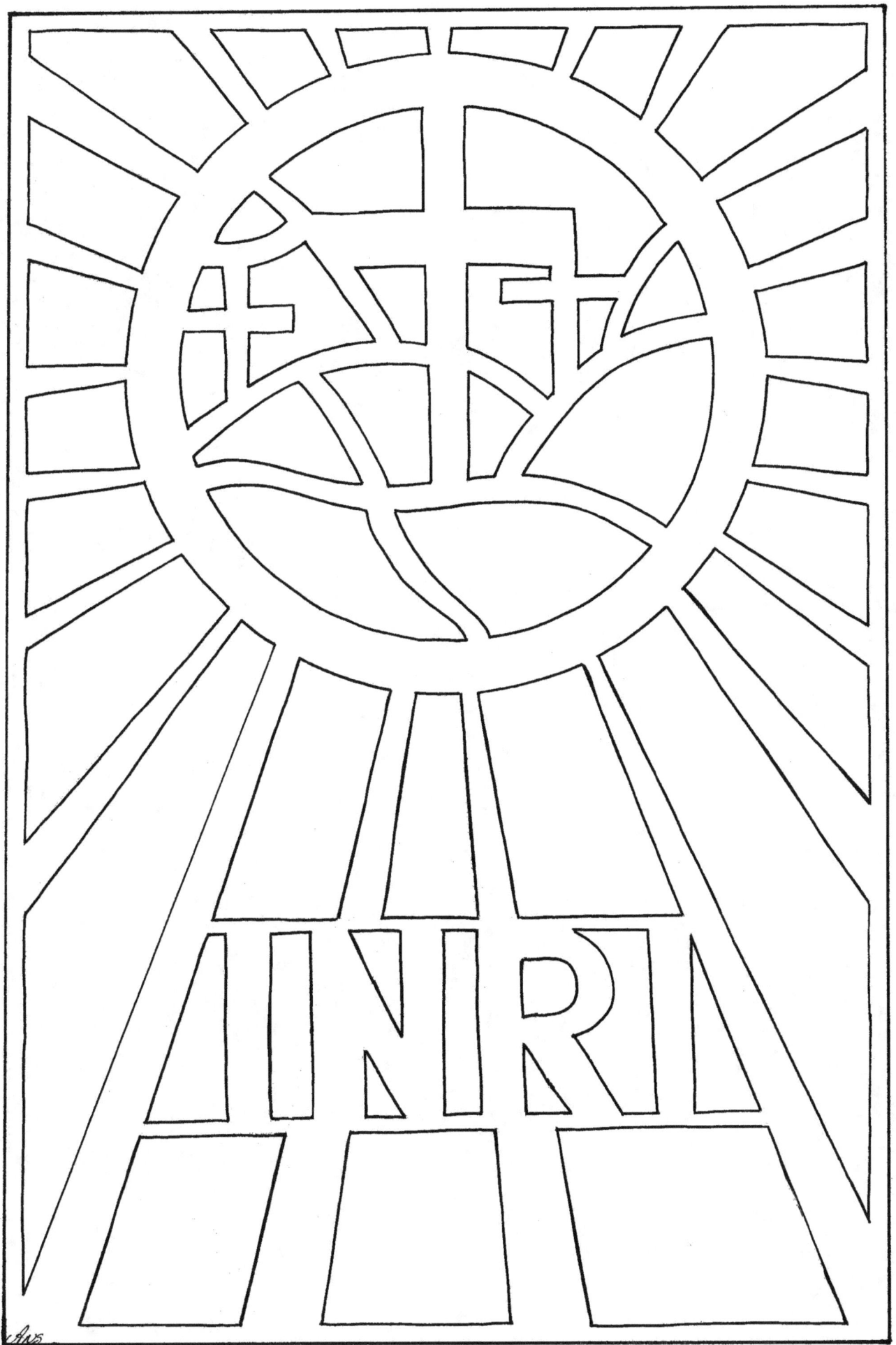

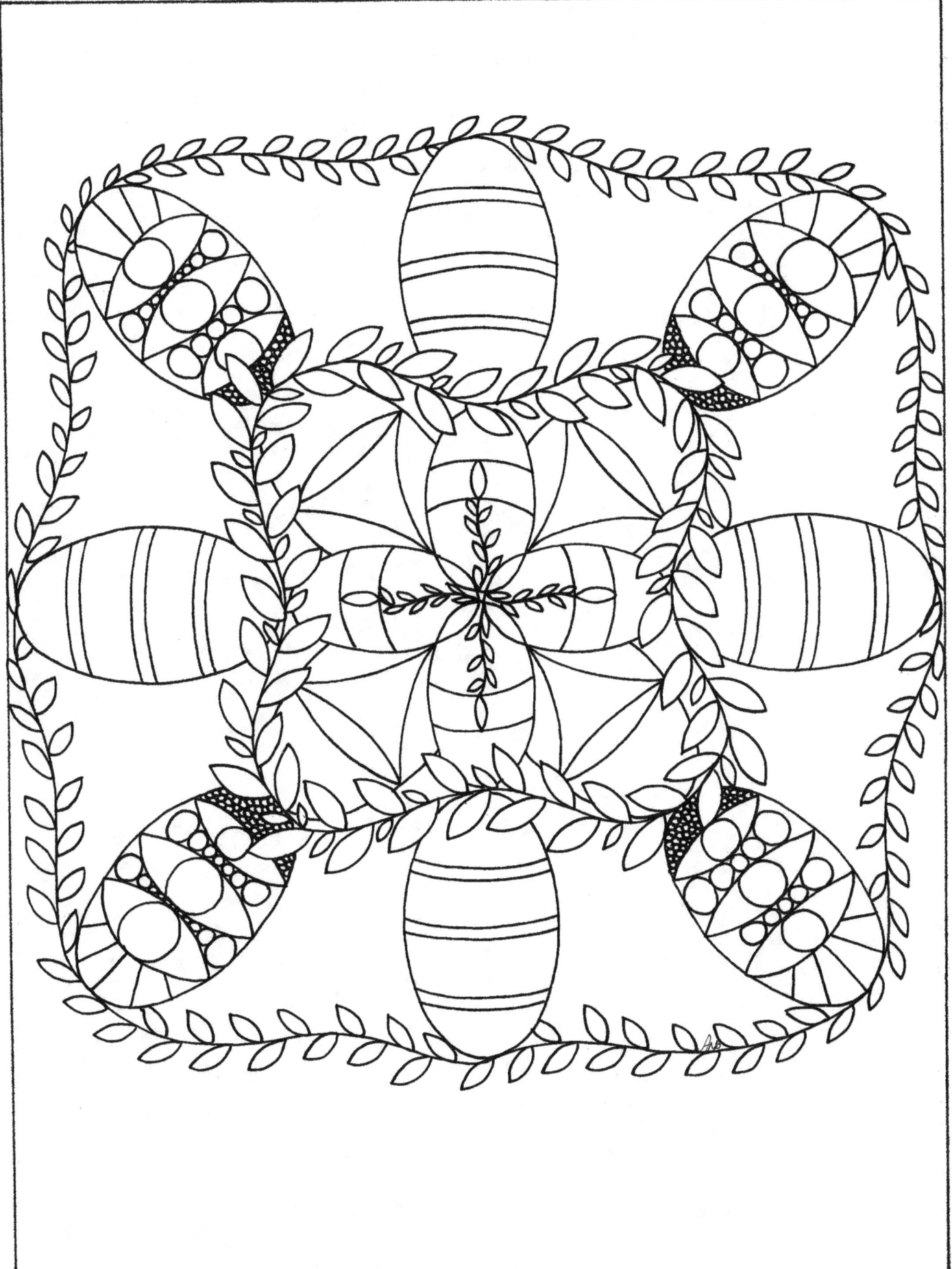

Contributing Artist
Jenny Wei
Taiwan

Facebook : zentangle fun

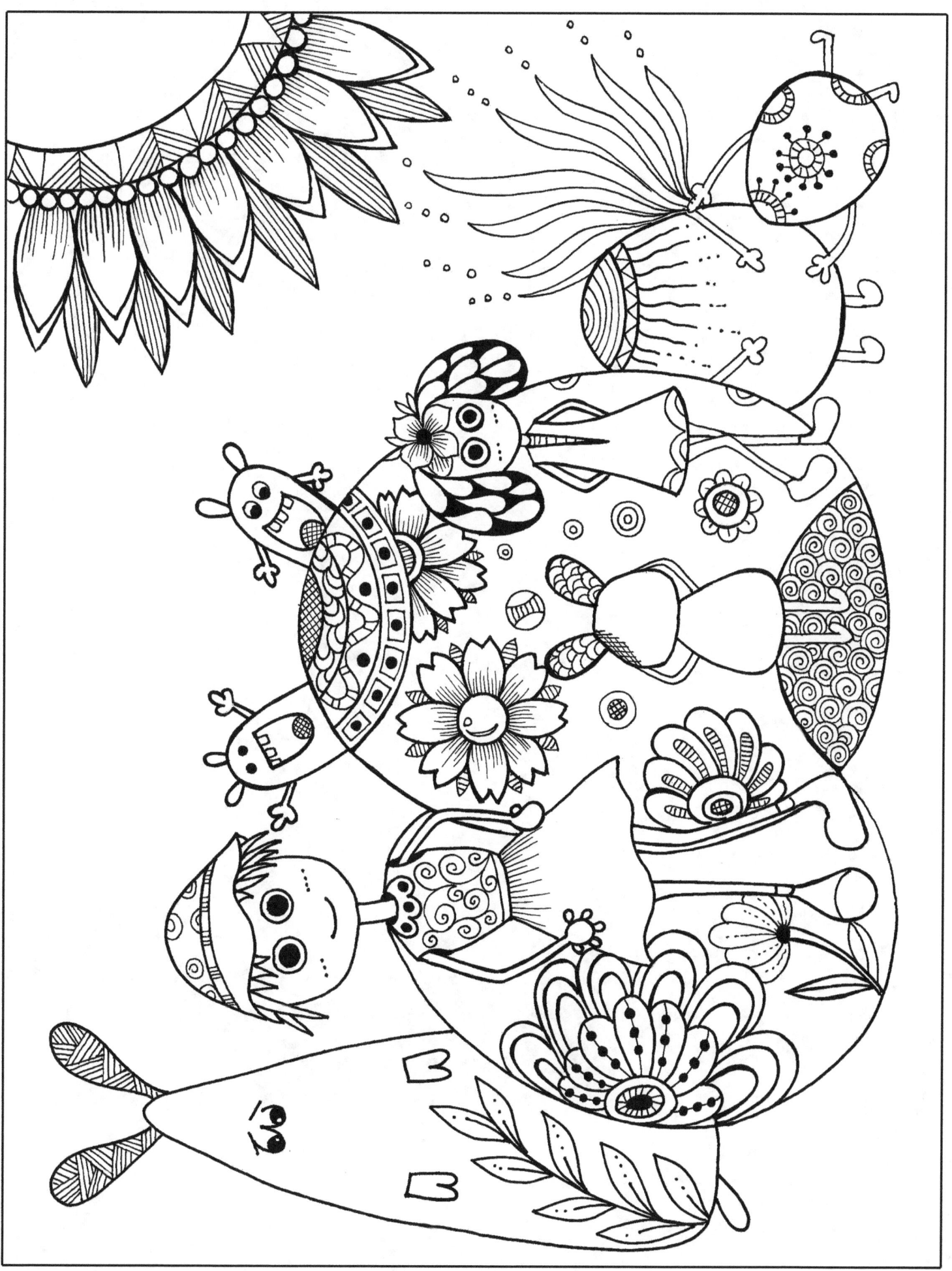

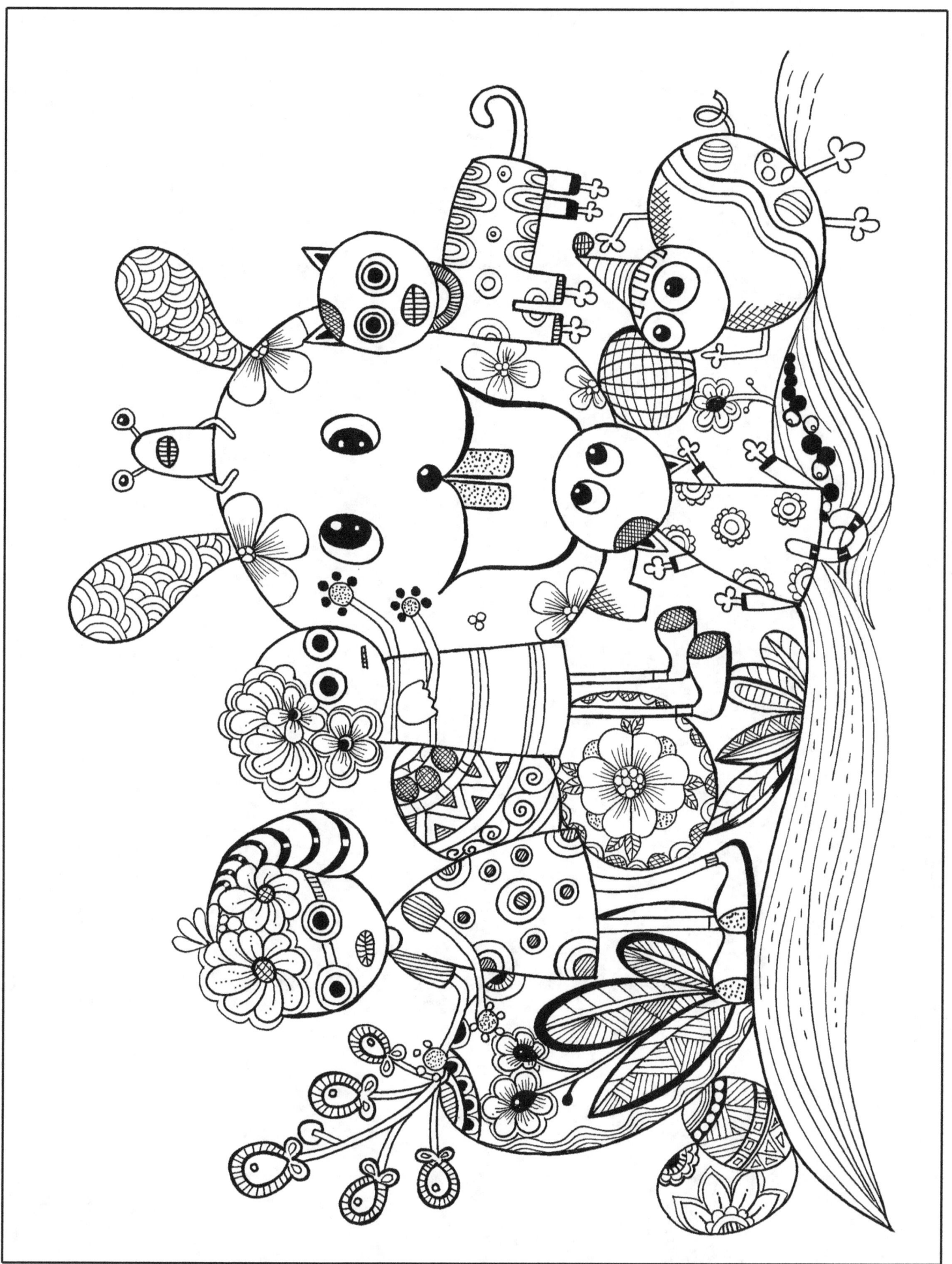

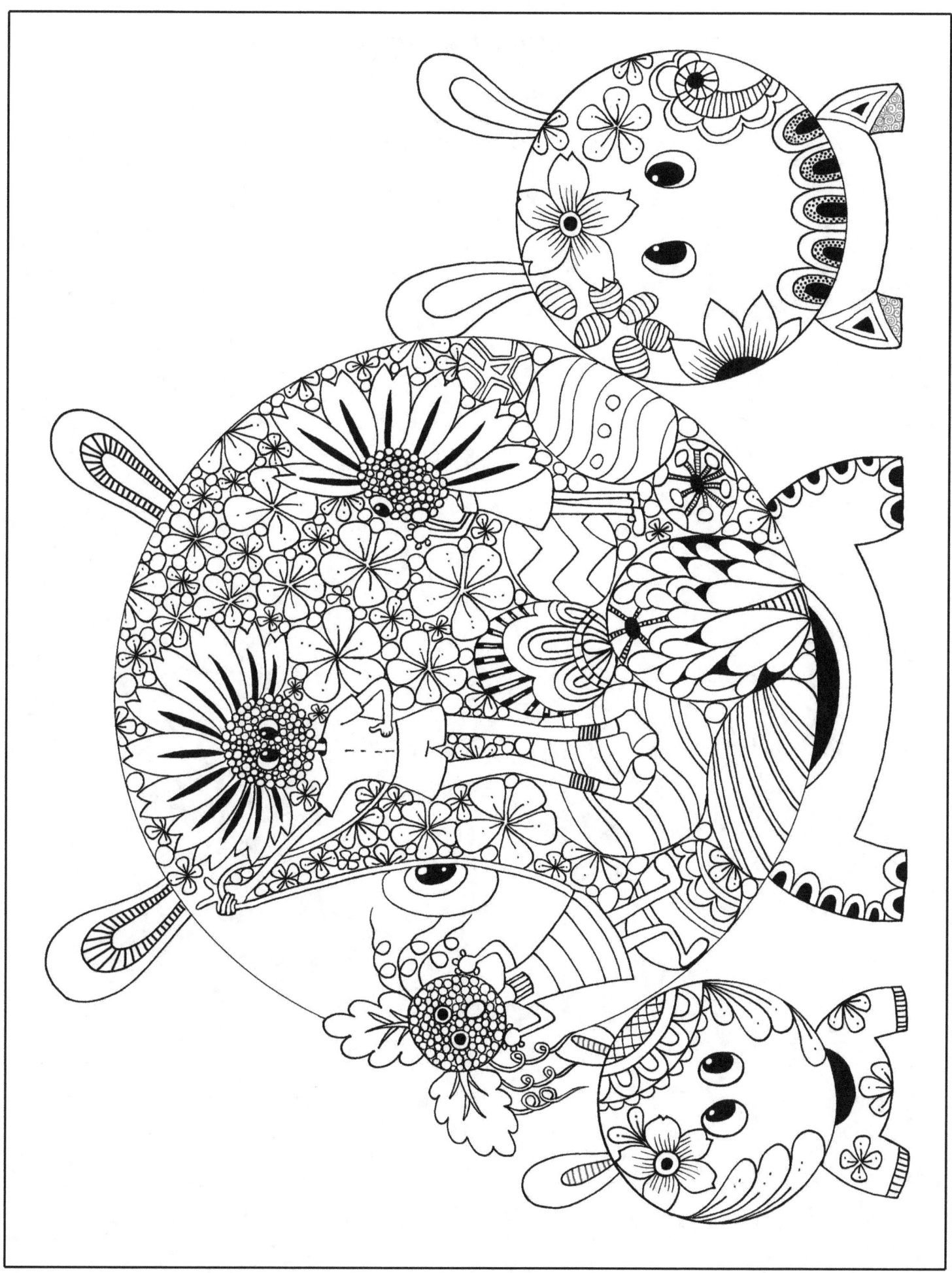

Contributing Artist
Audrey Sagh
Saskatoon, Saskatchewan Canada

Facebook : AMS-Artwork

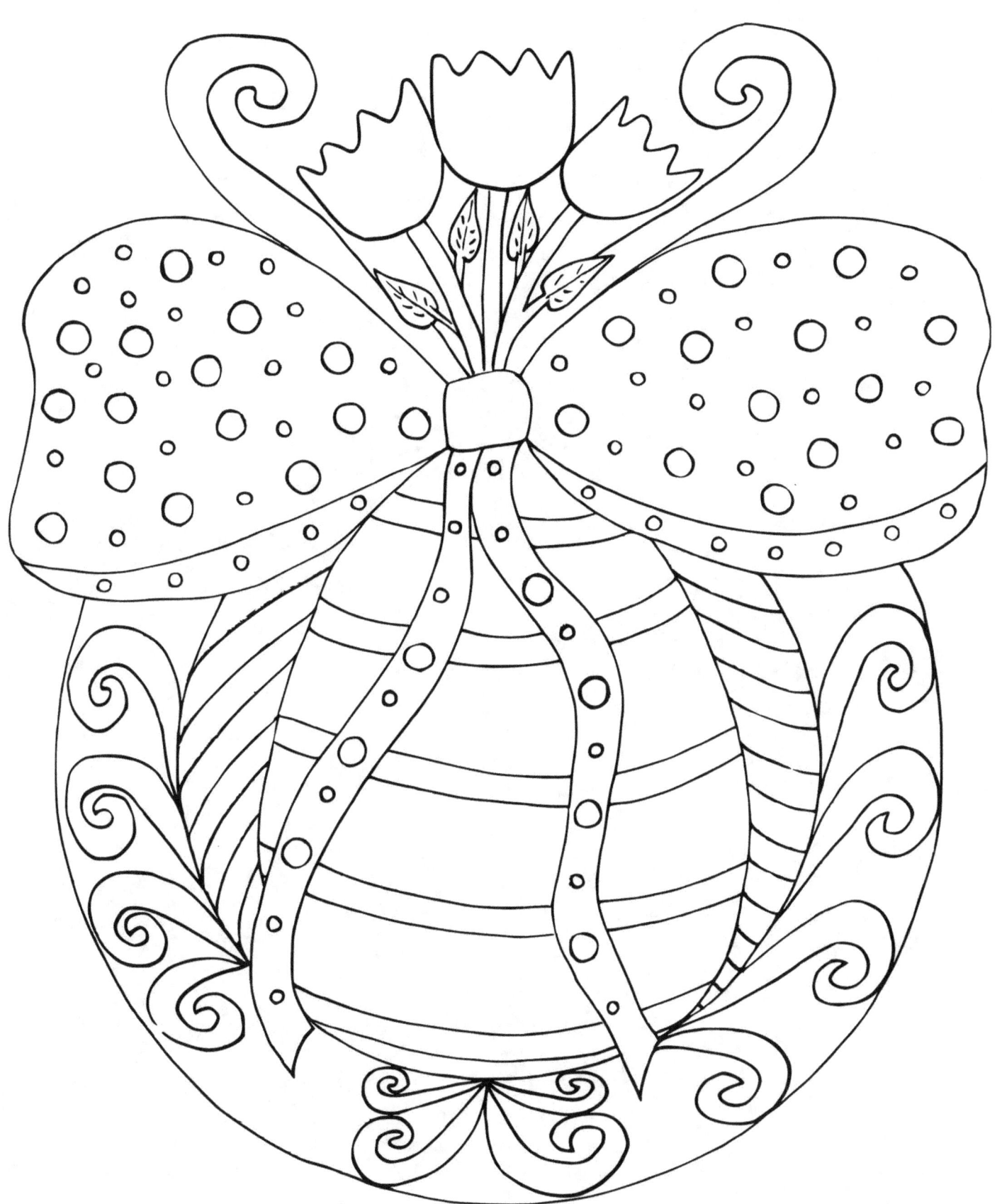

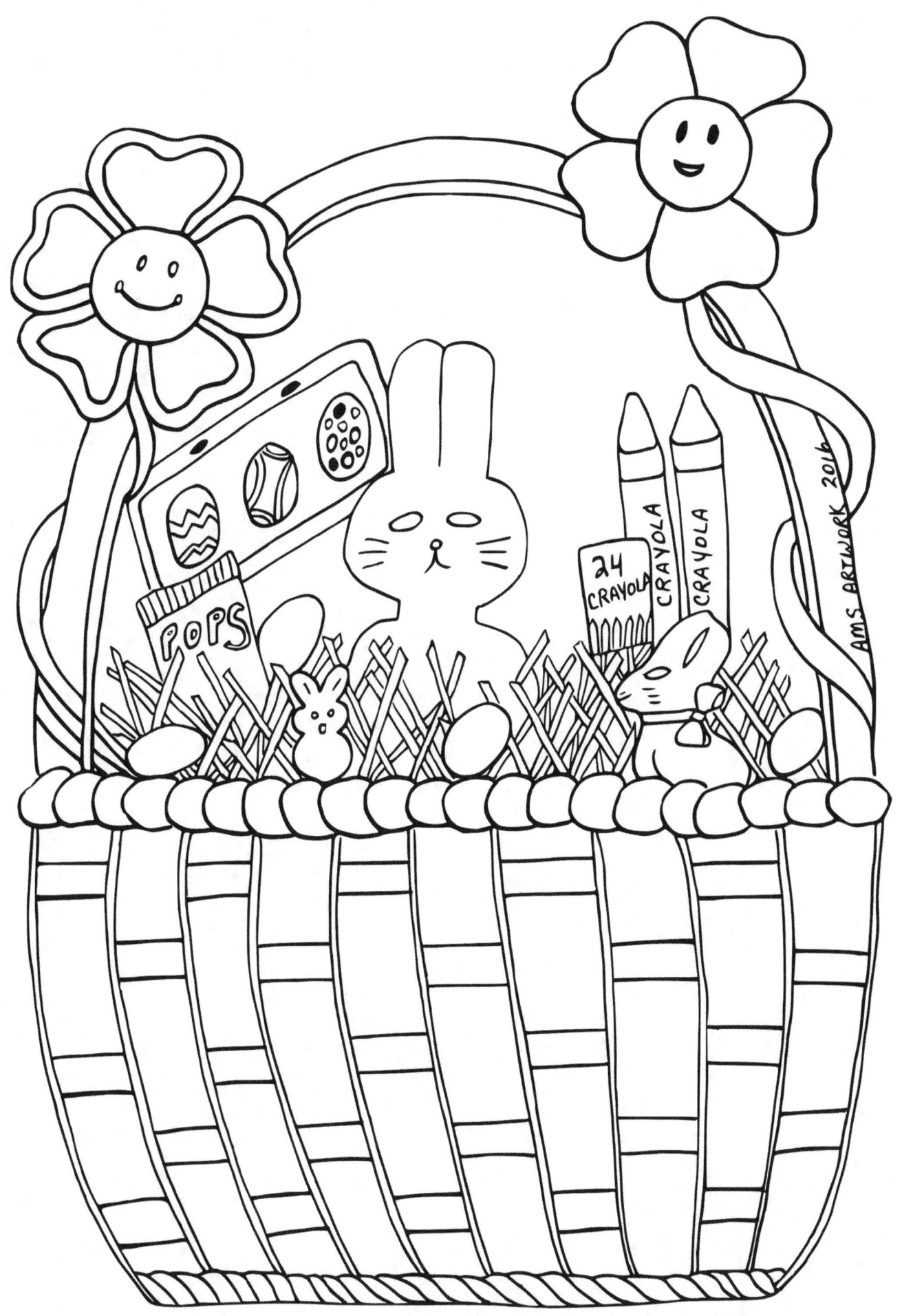

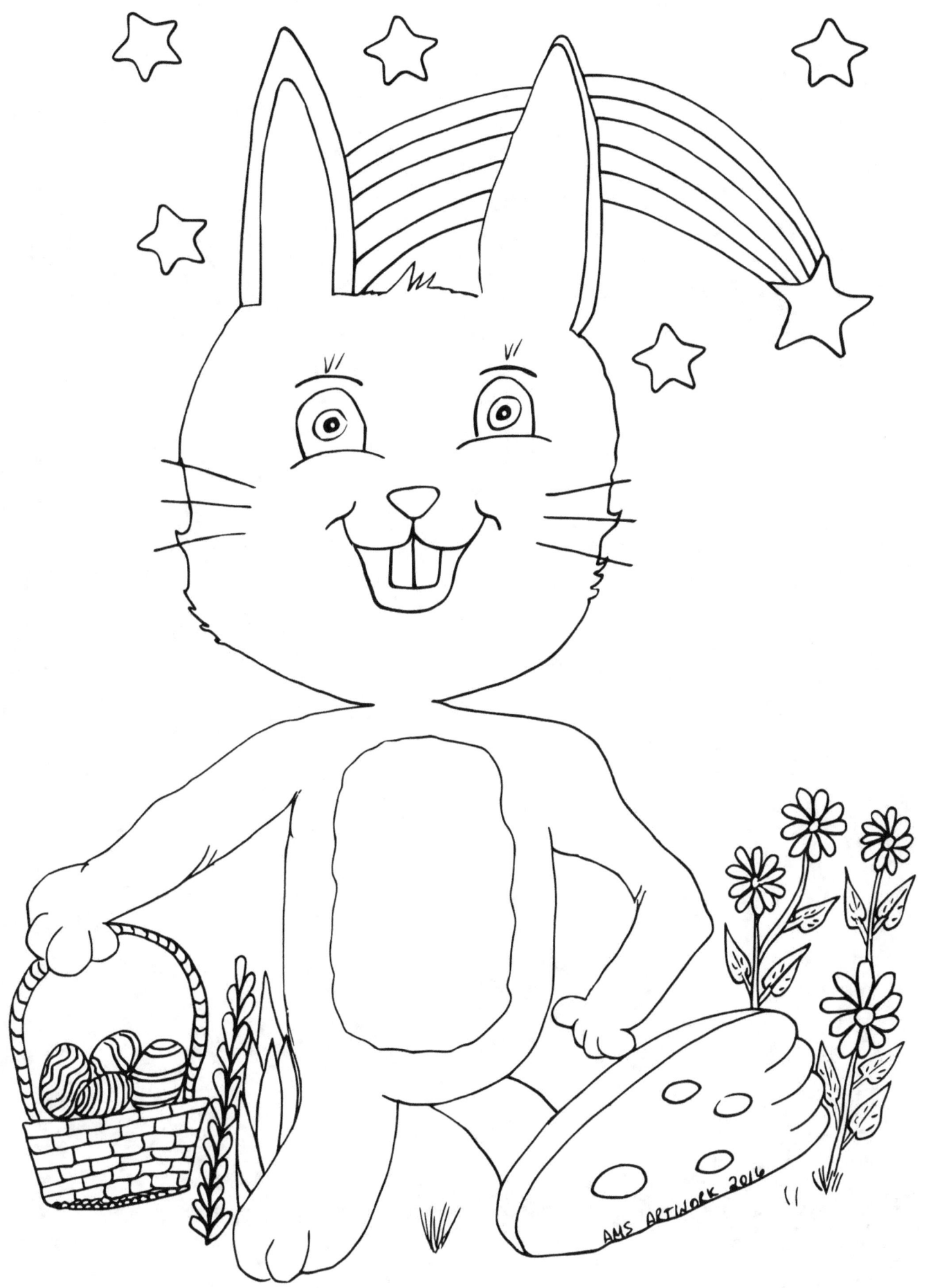

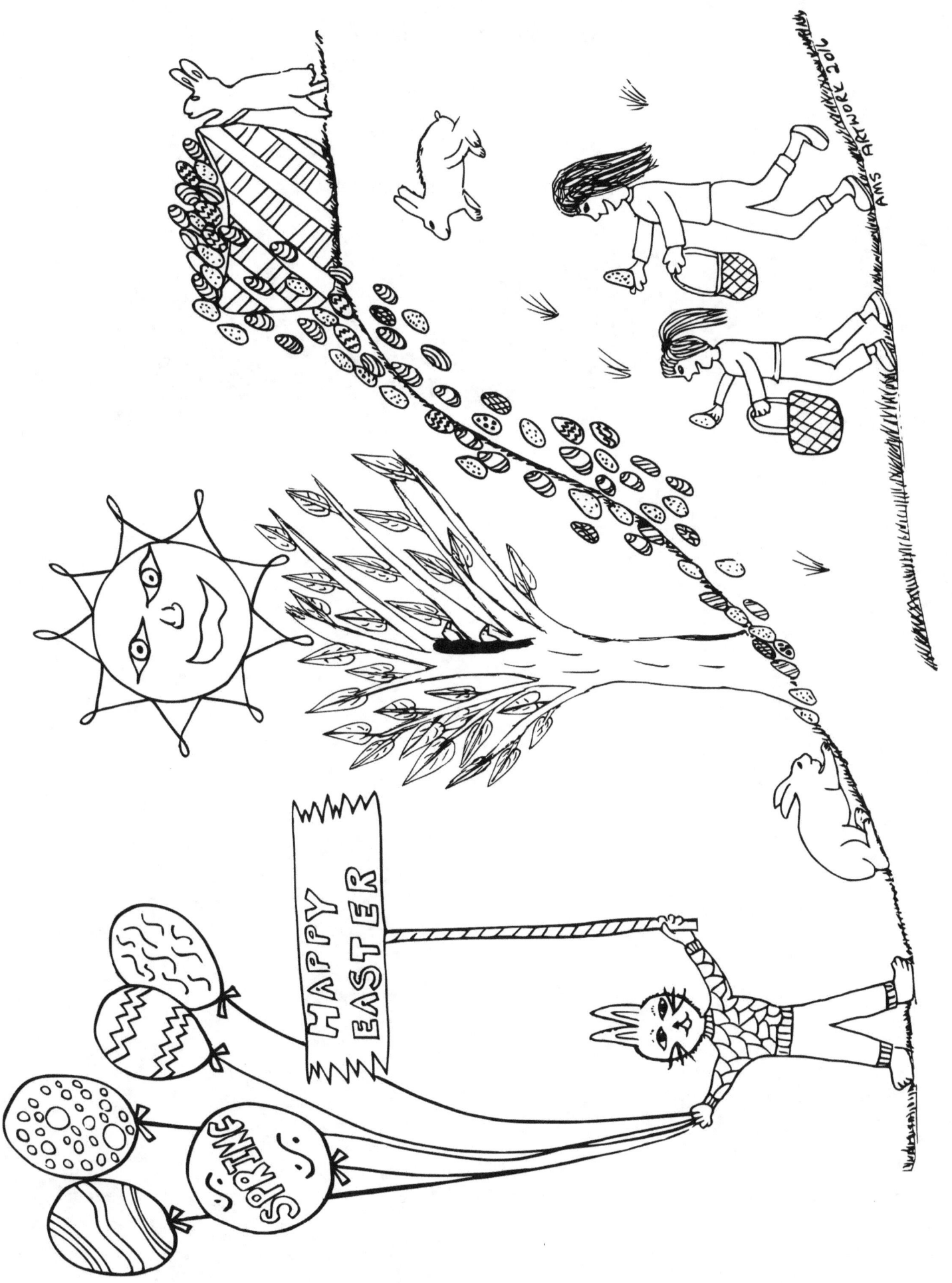

Contributing Artist
Arianne Schimmel
The Netherlands

Facebook : ArianneSchimmel

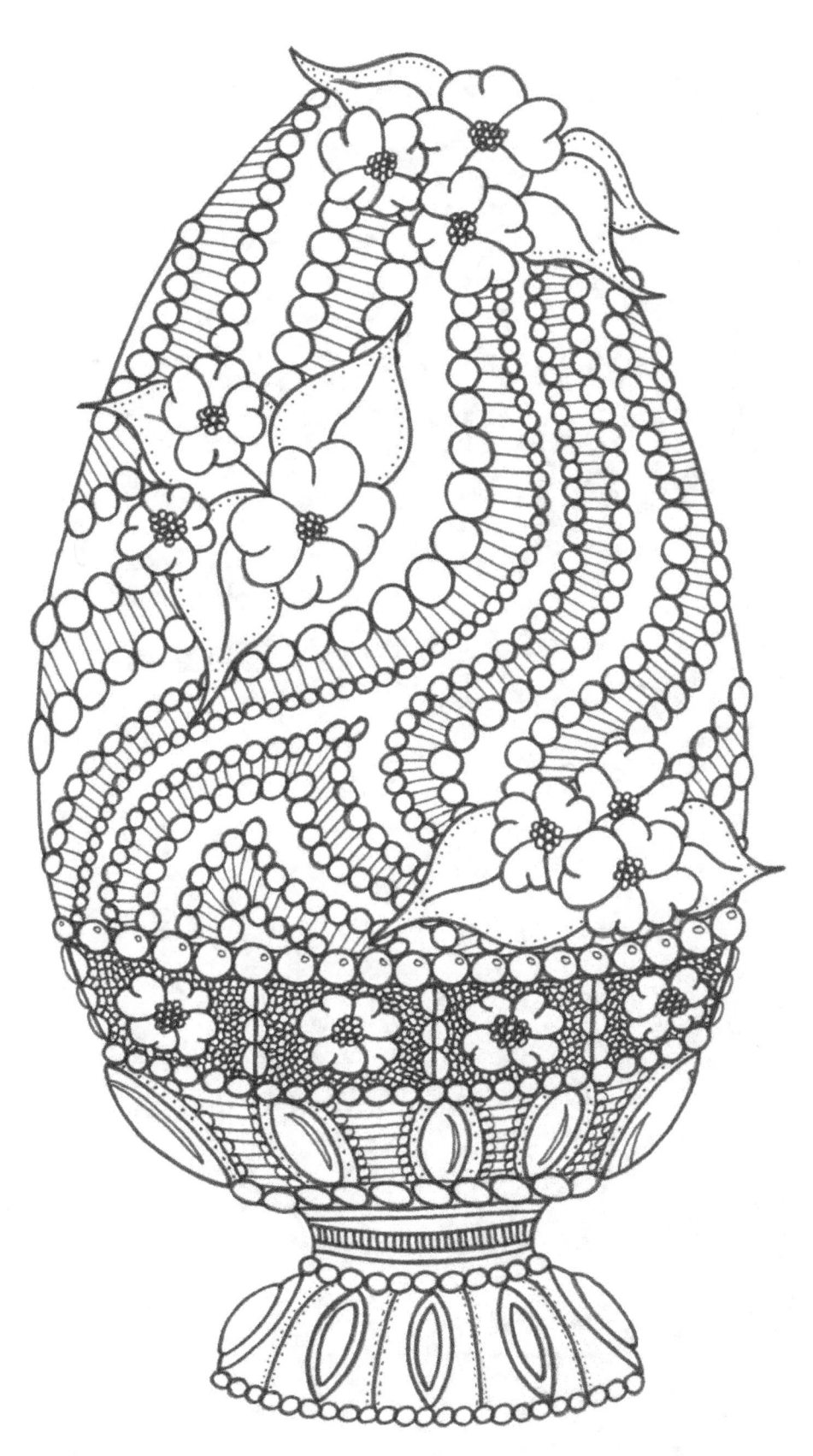

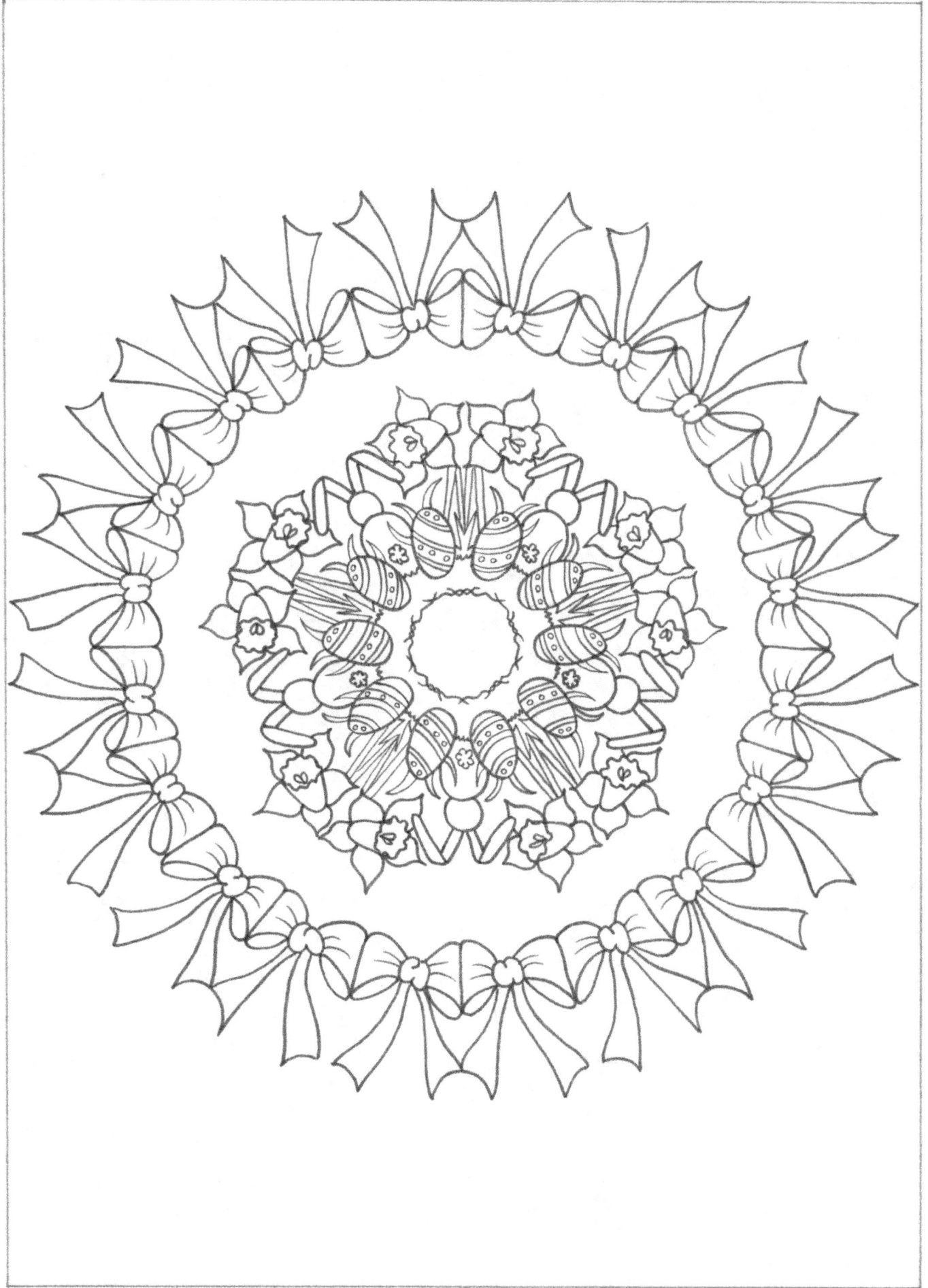

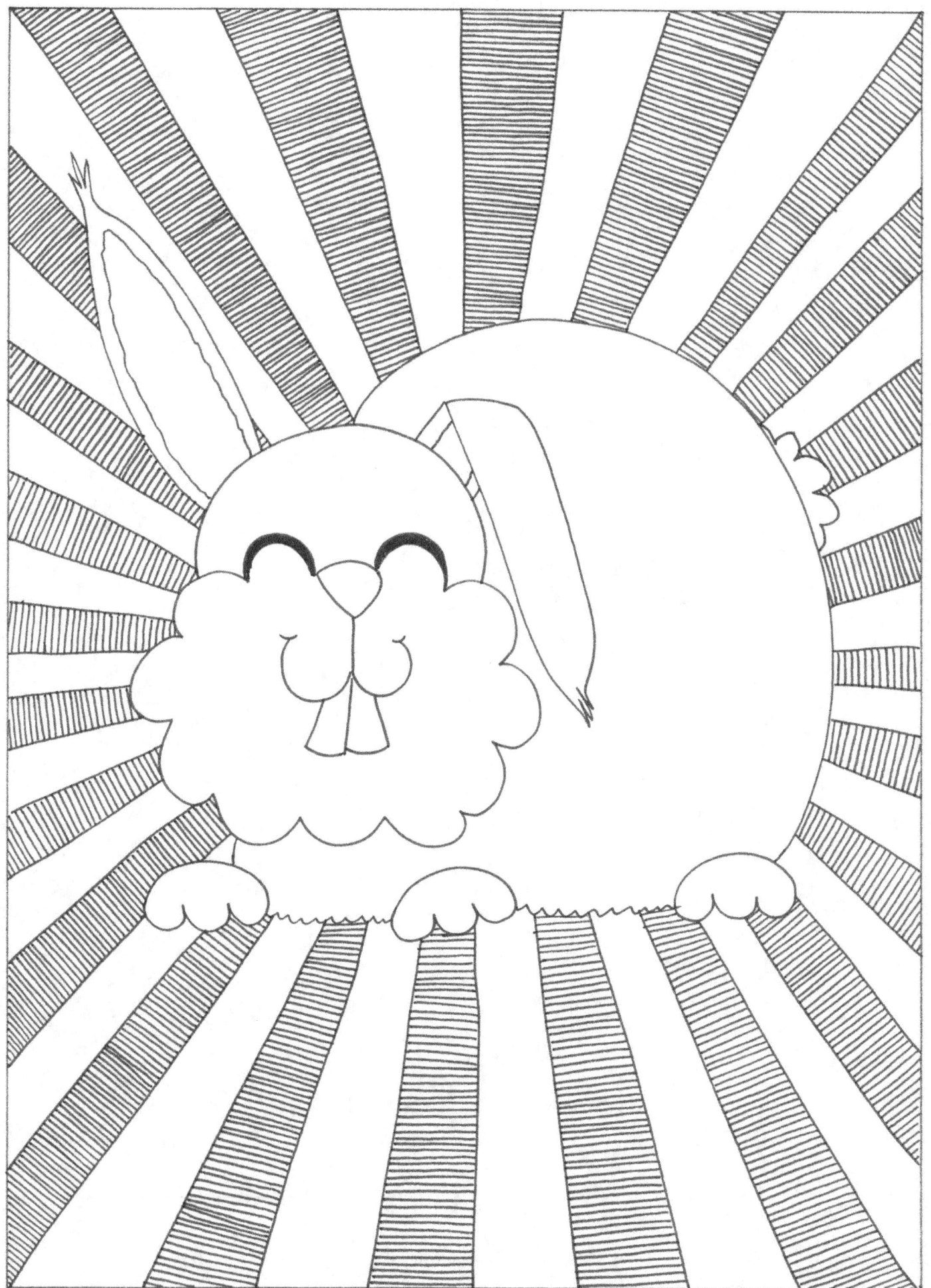

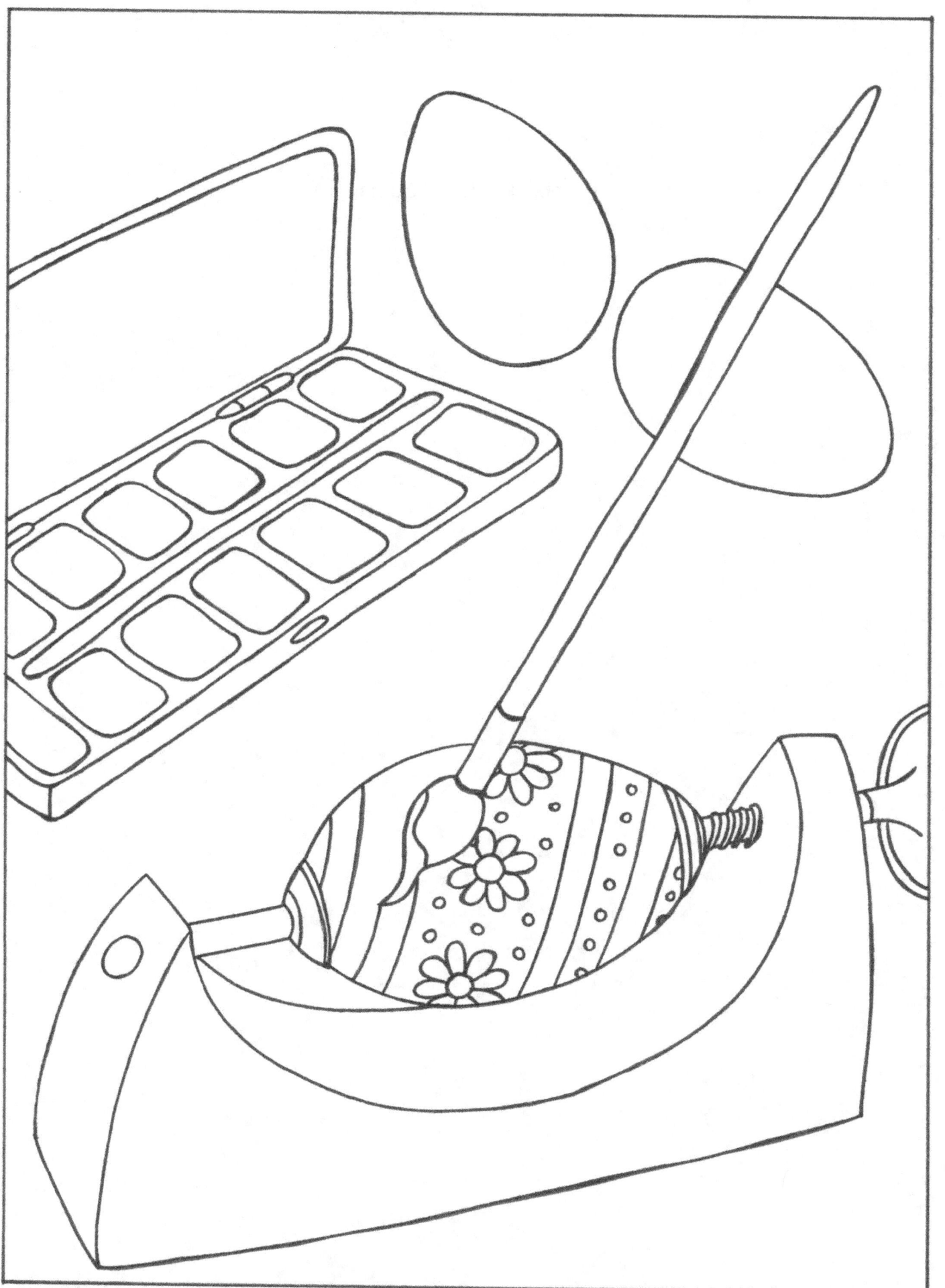

Contributing Artist
T.J.
USA

Facebook : TJsArtCorner

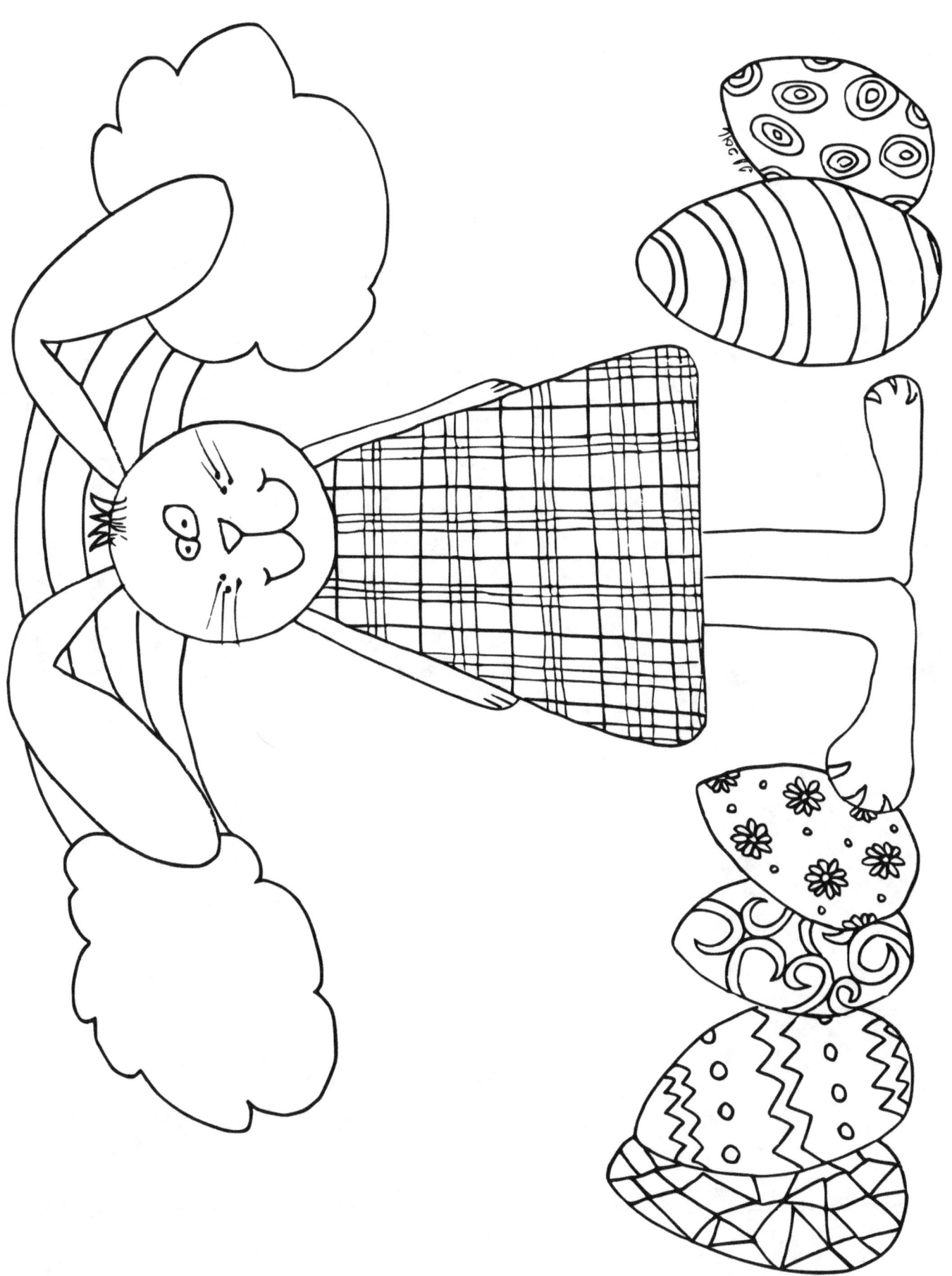

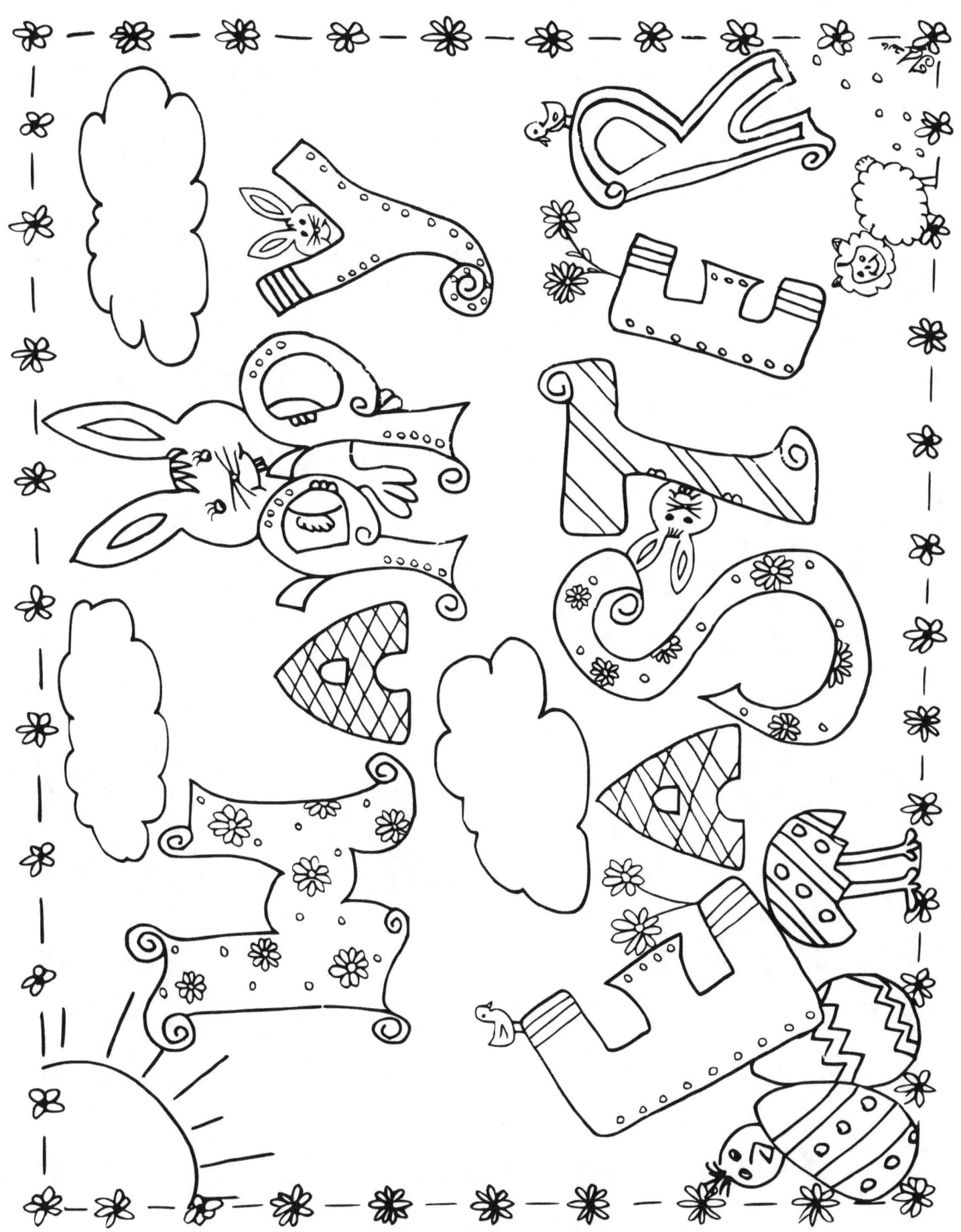

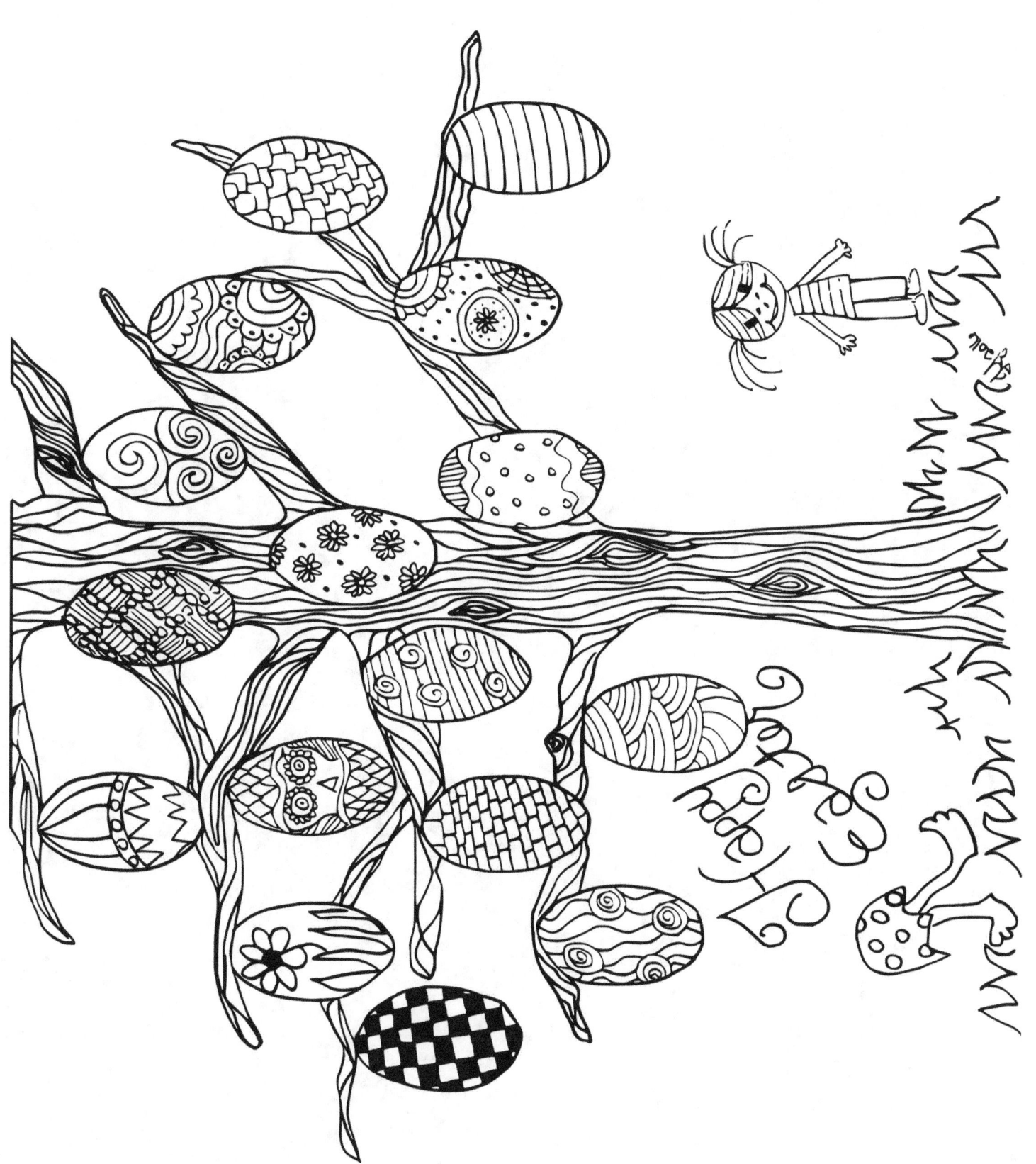

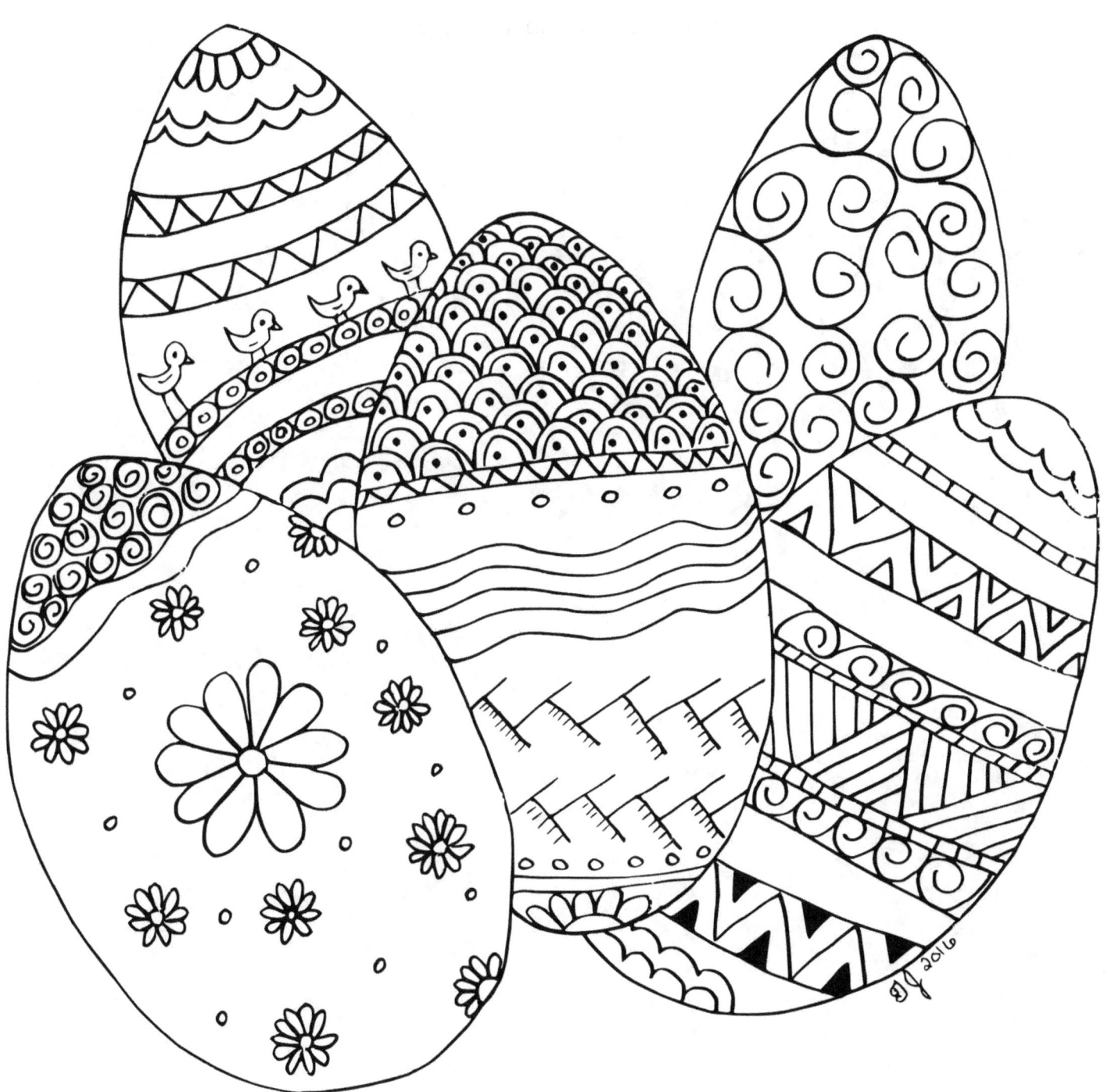

Contributing Artist
Inge Boogaers-Kanters
The Netherlands

Facebook : artstudiopimpoem

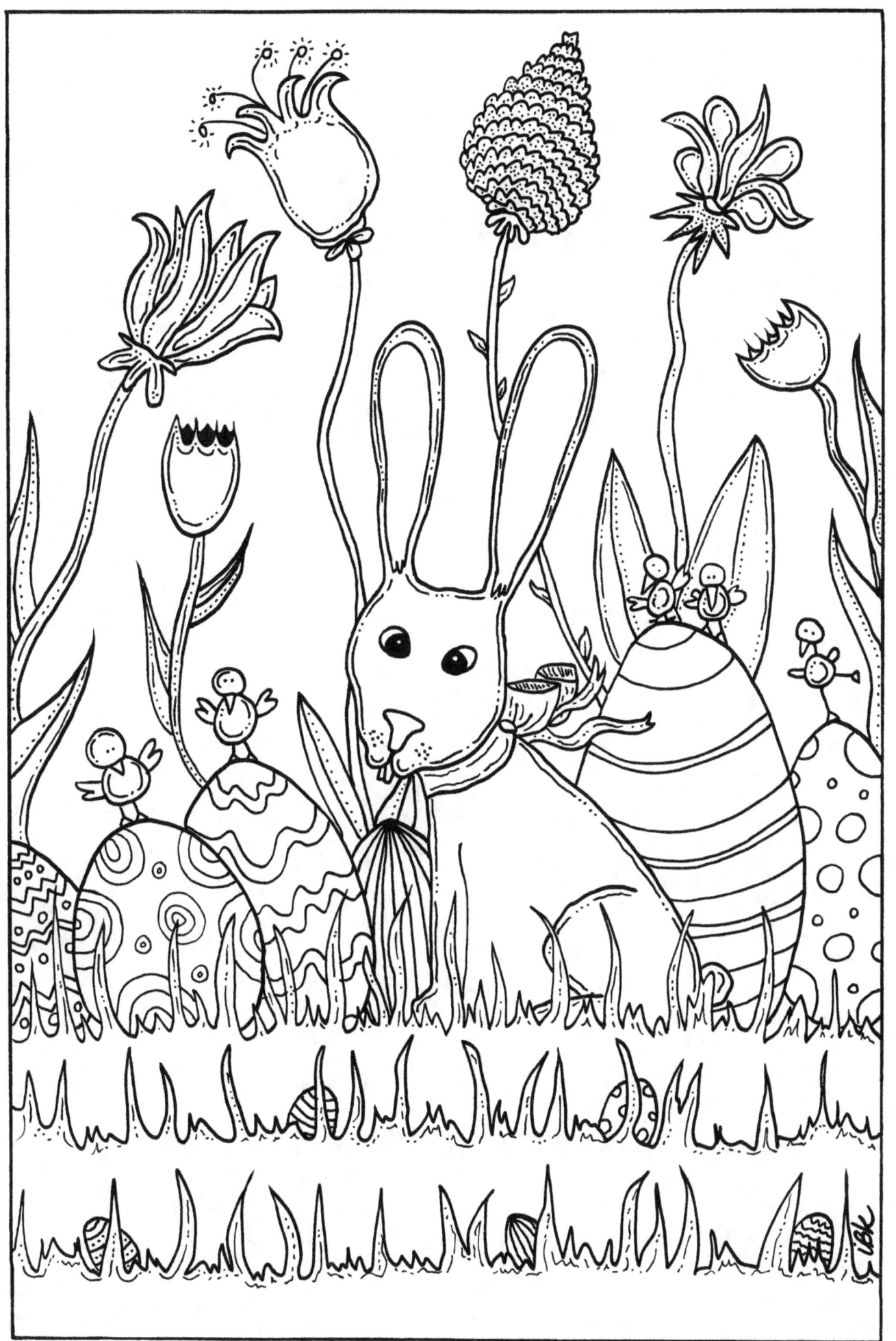

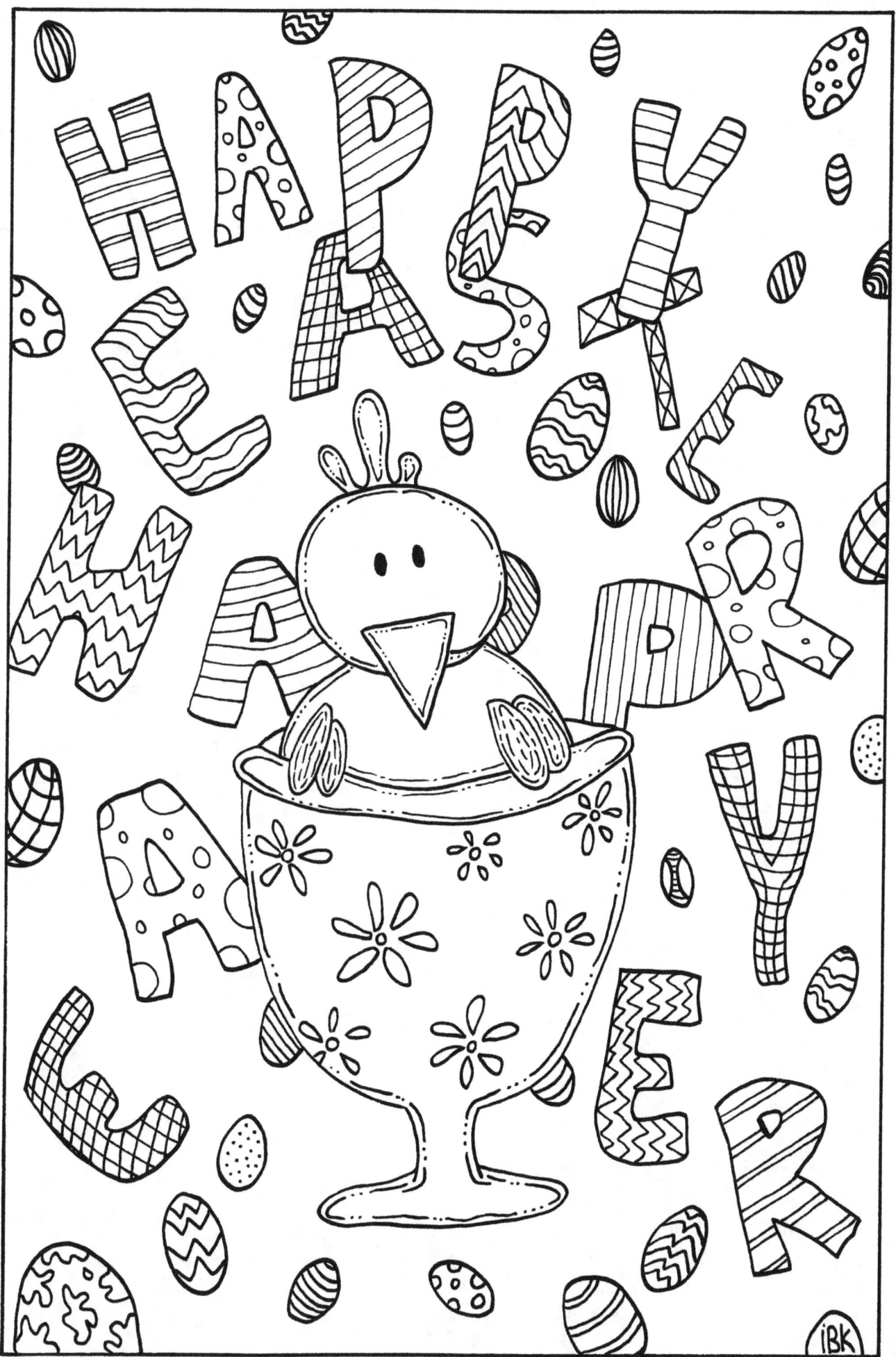

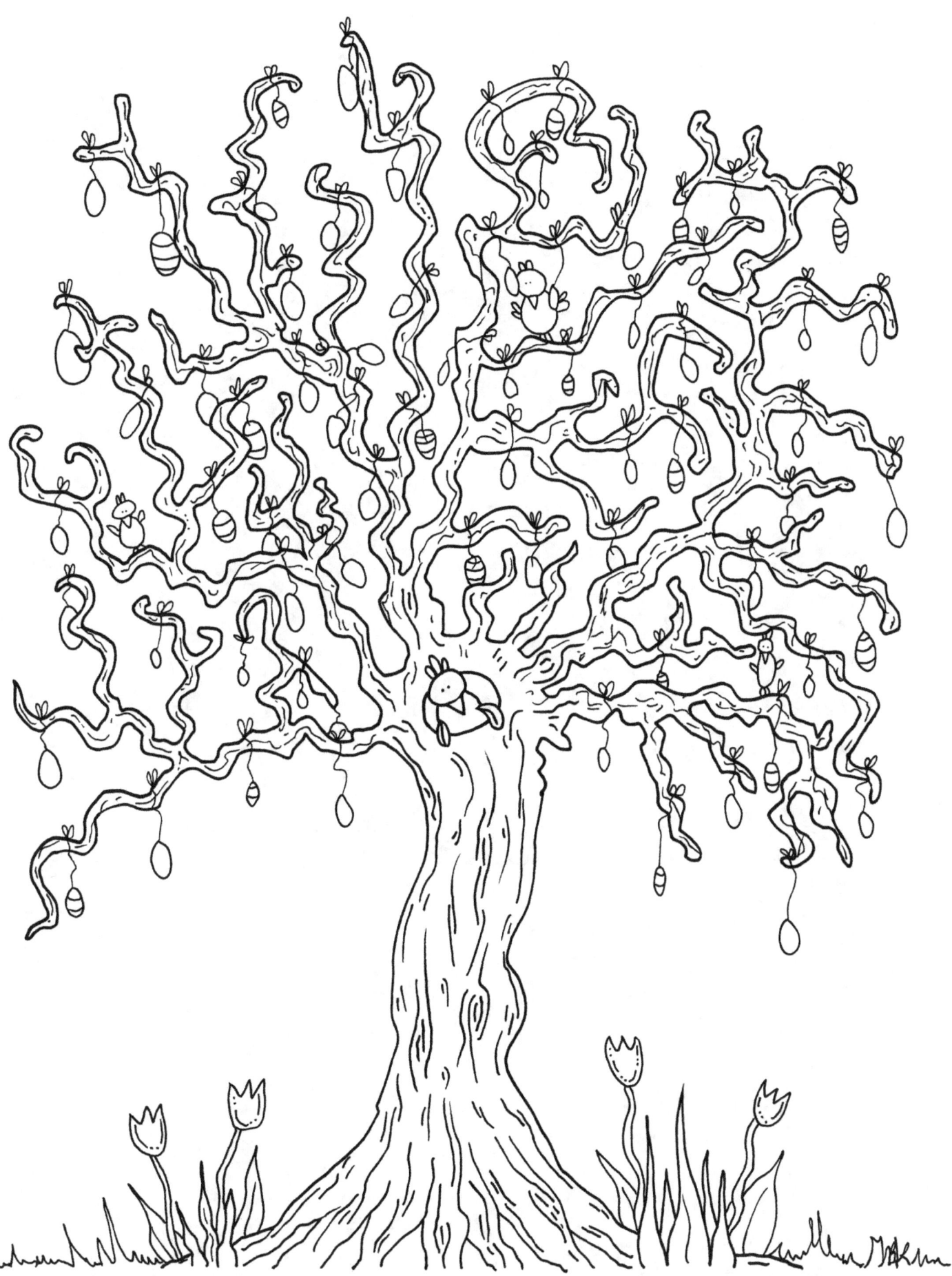

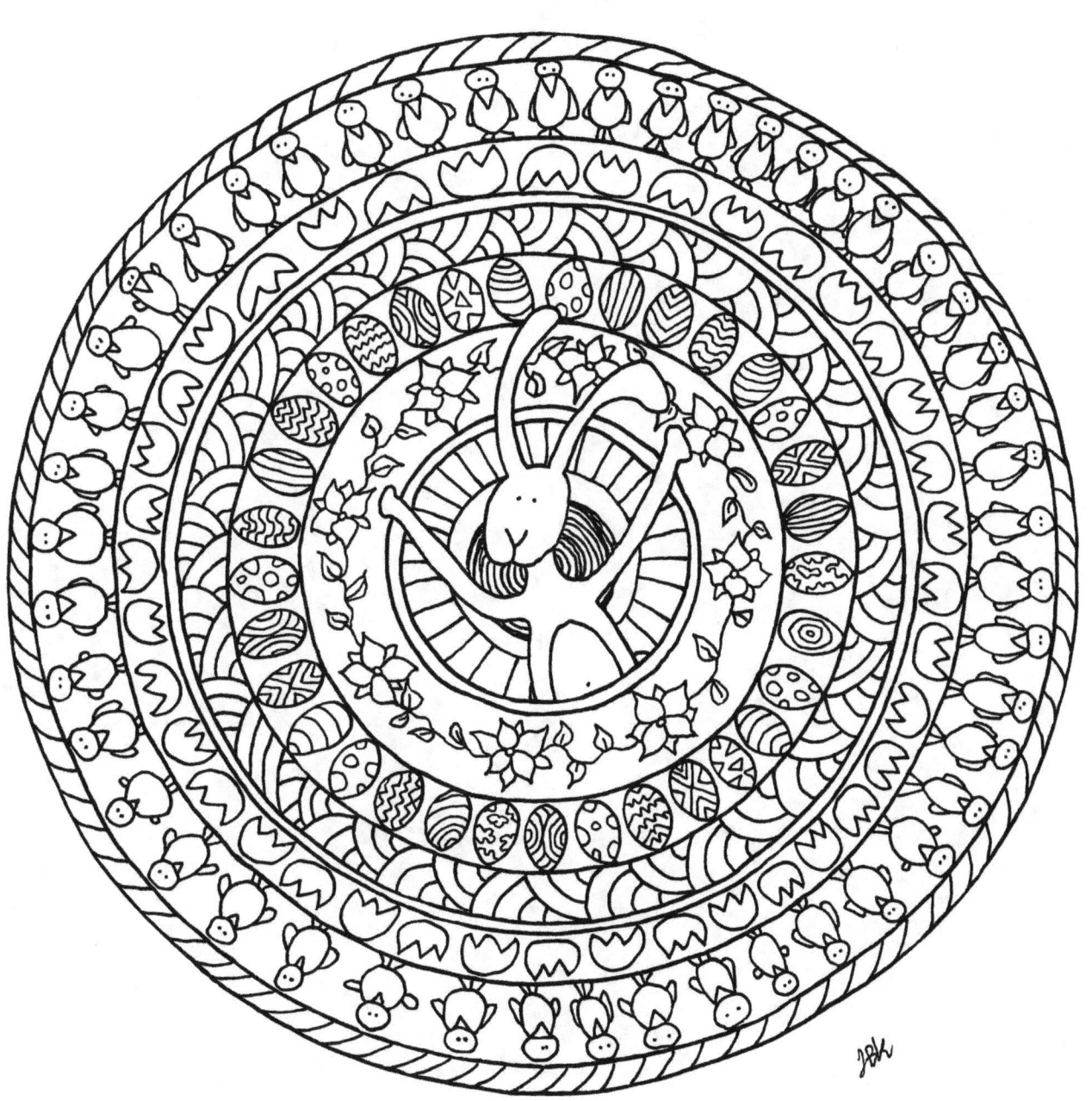

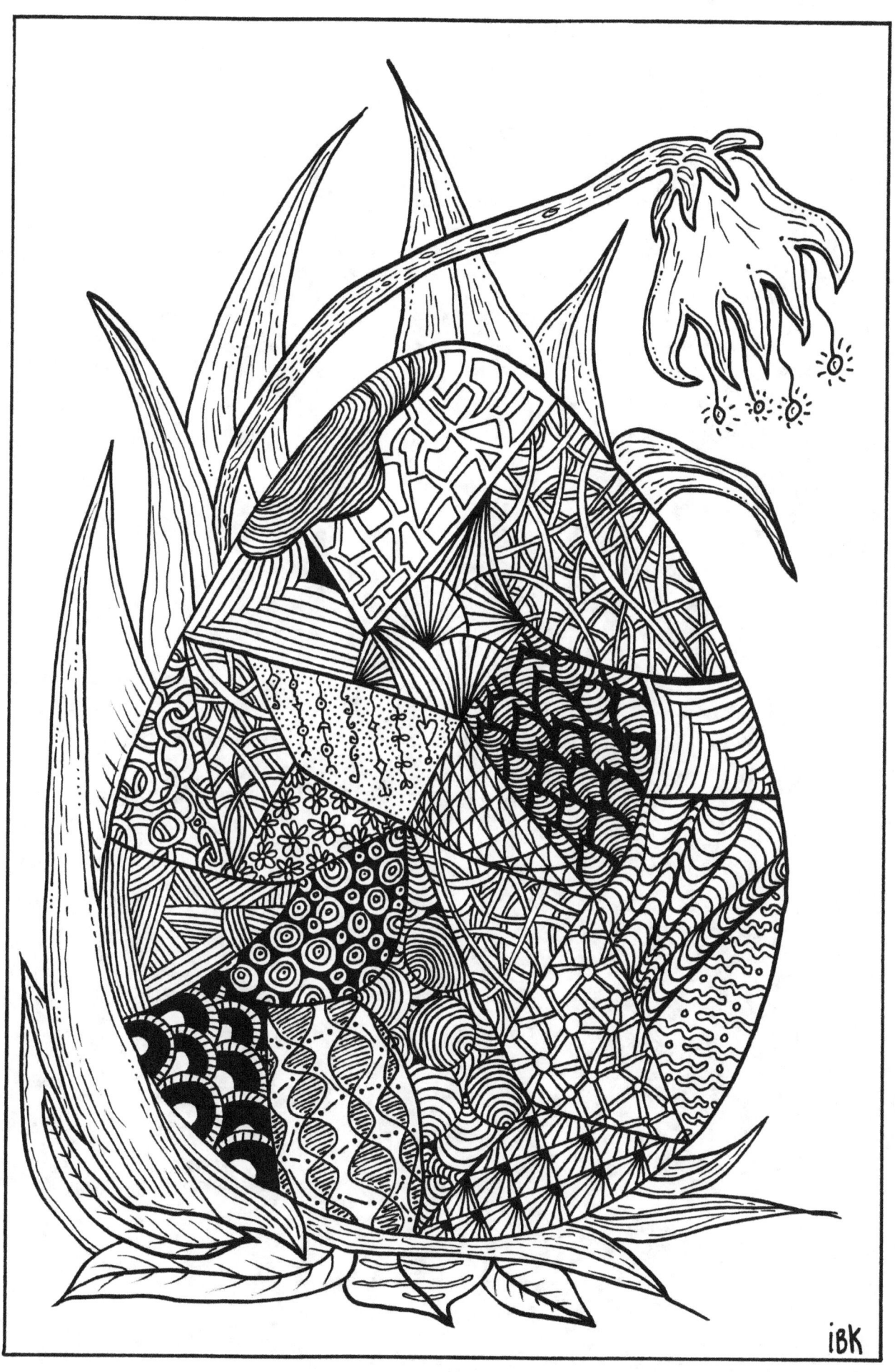

Contributing Artist
Pica Wu
Taiwan

Facebook : Pica's Zentangle Art

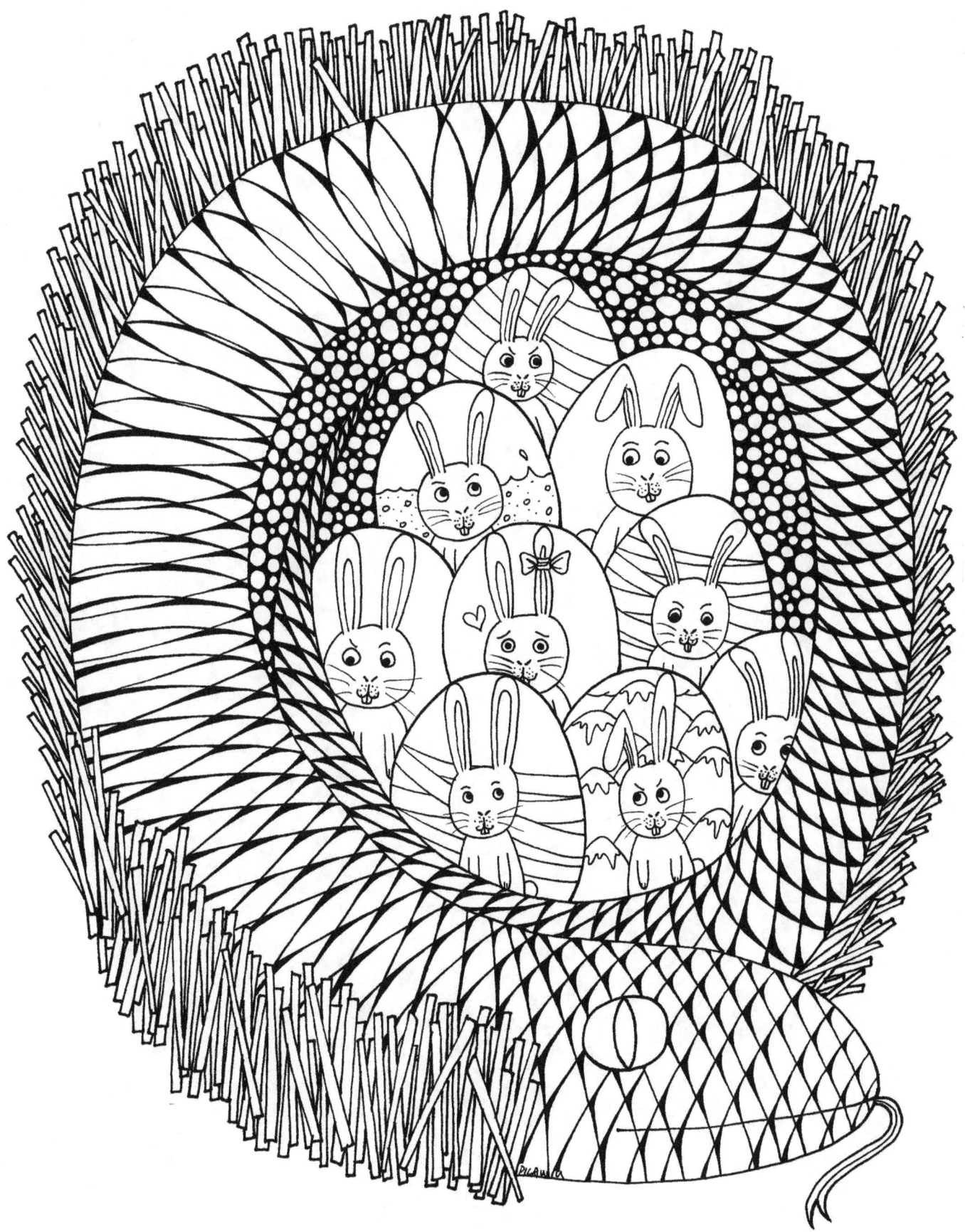

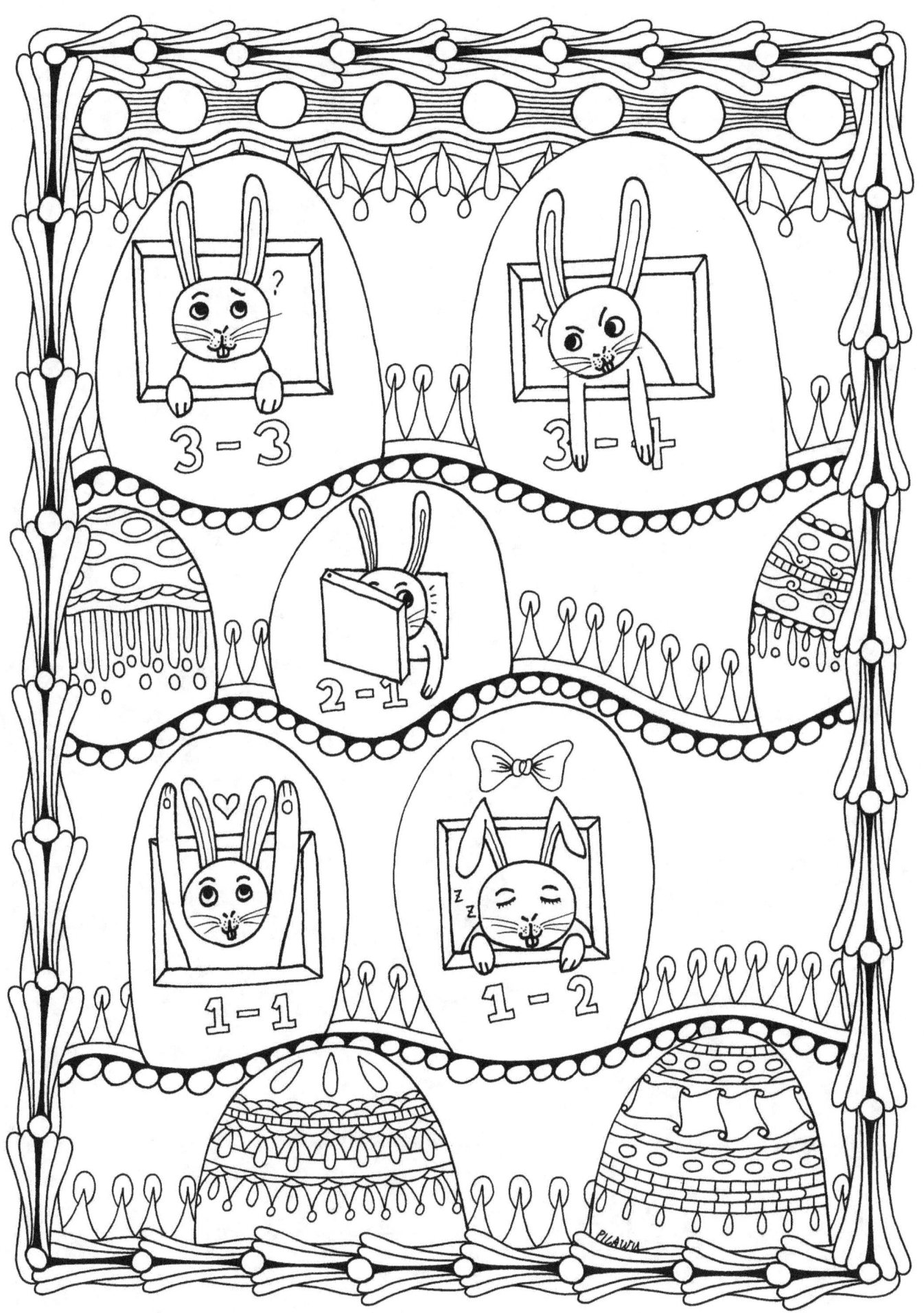

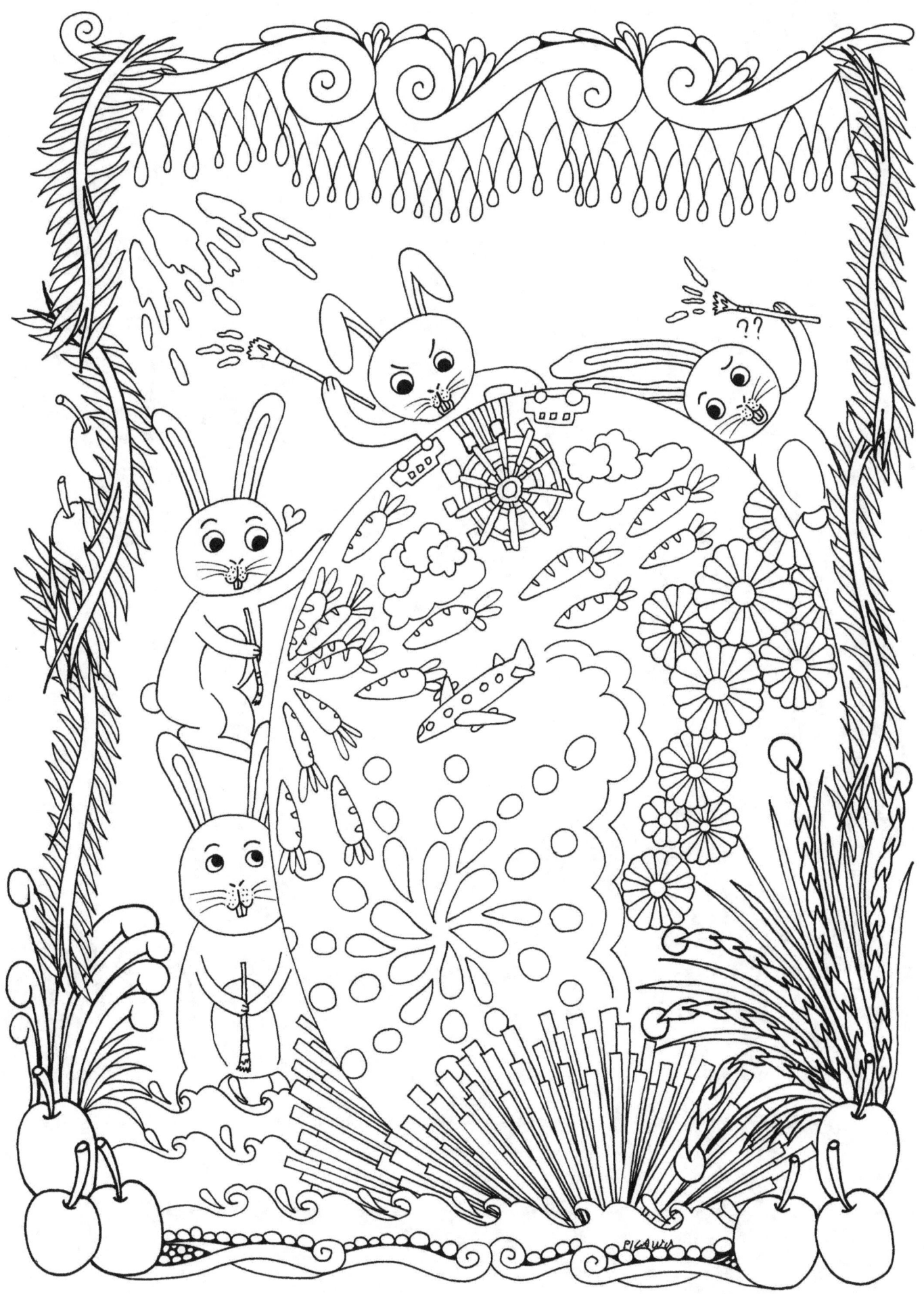

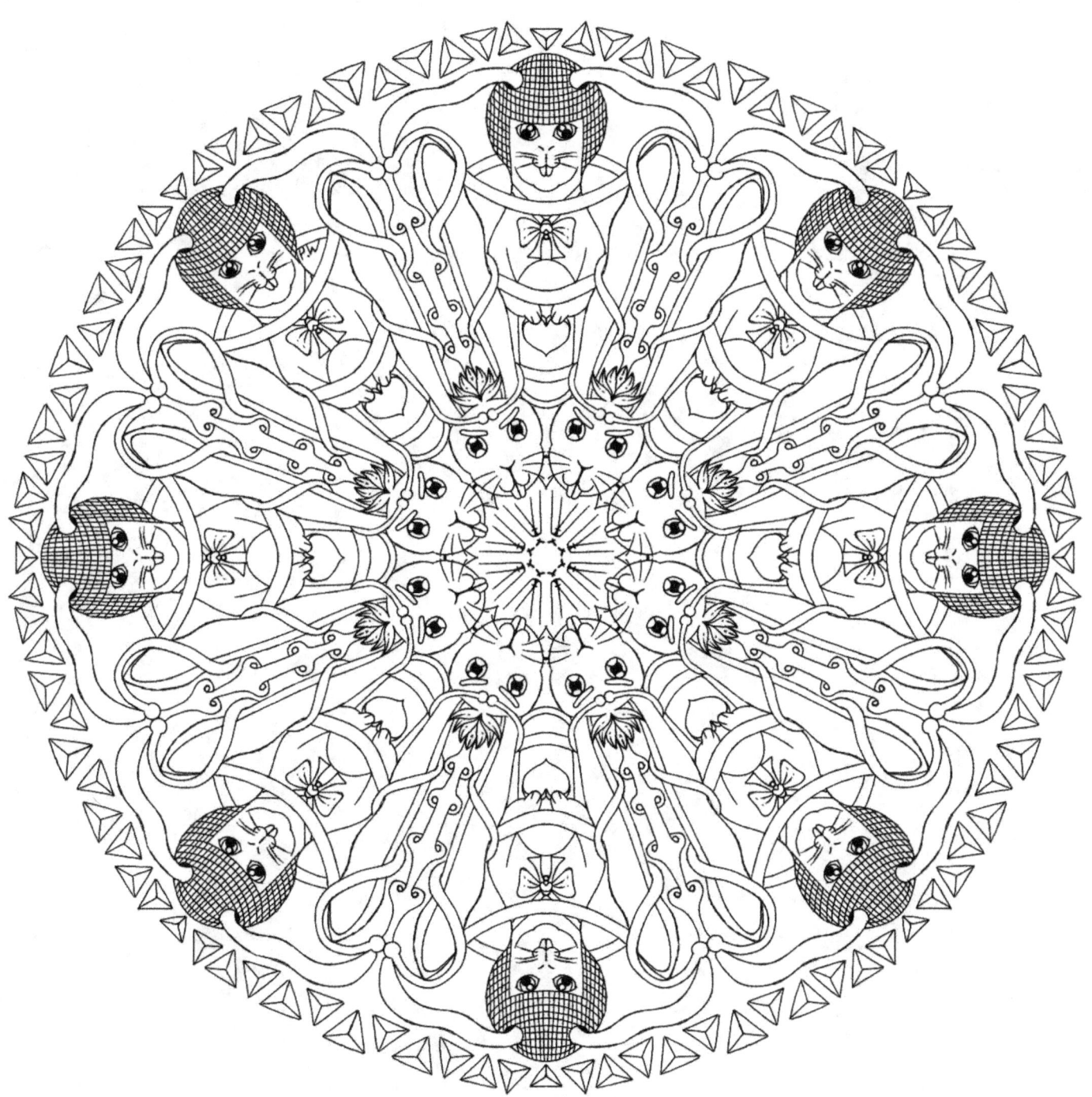

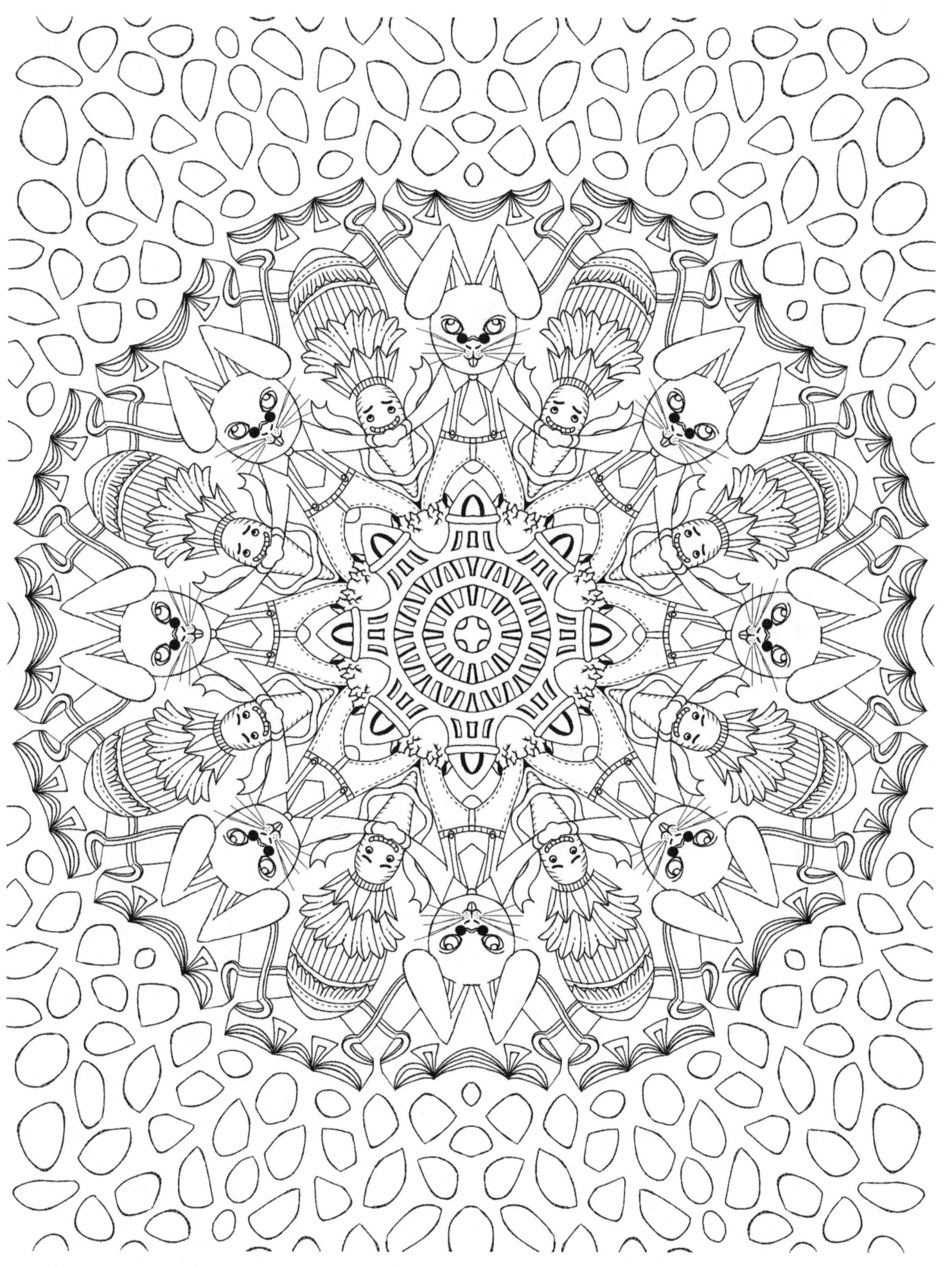

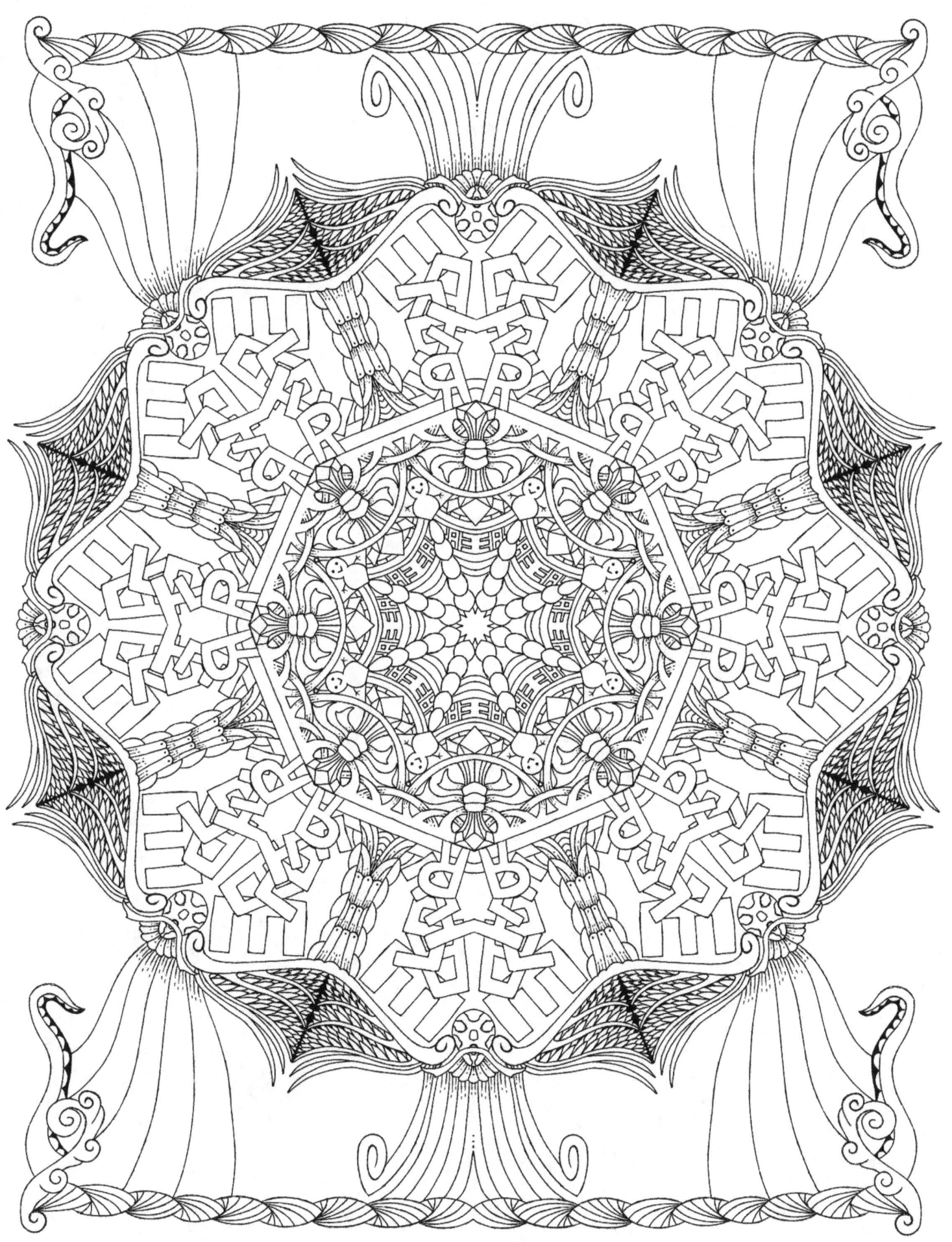

Contributing Artist
Rover Hsiao
Taiwan

Facebook : roverhsiao2015

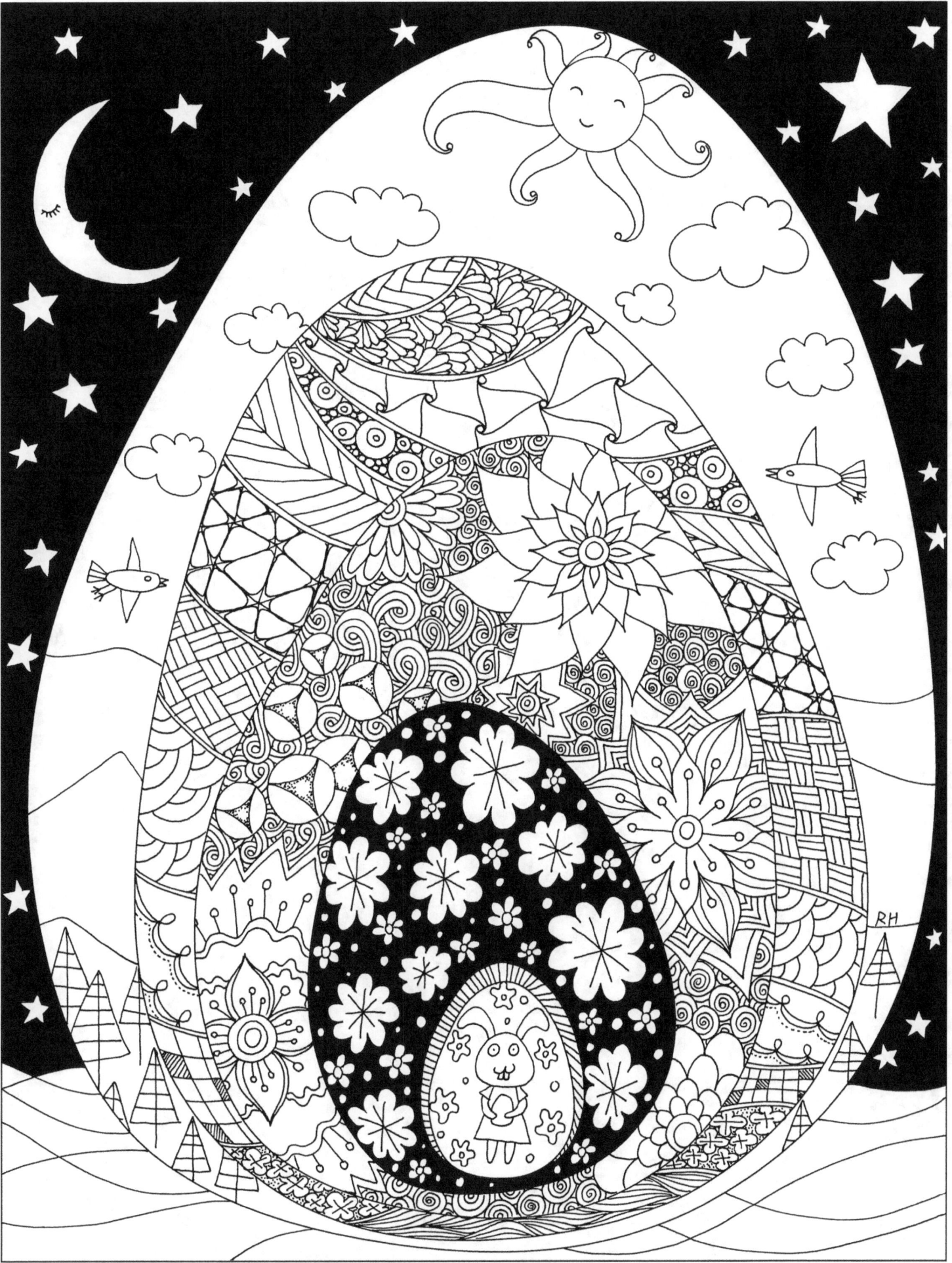

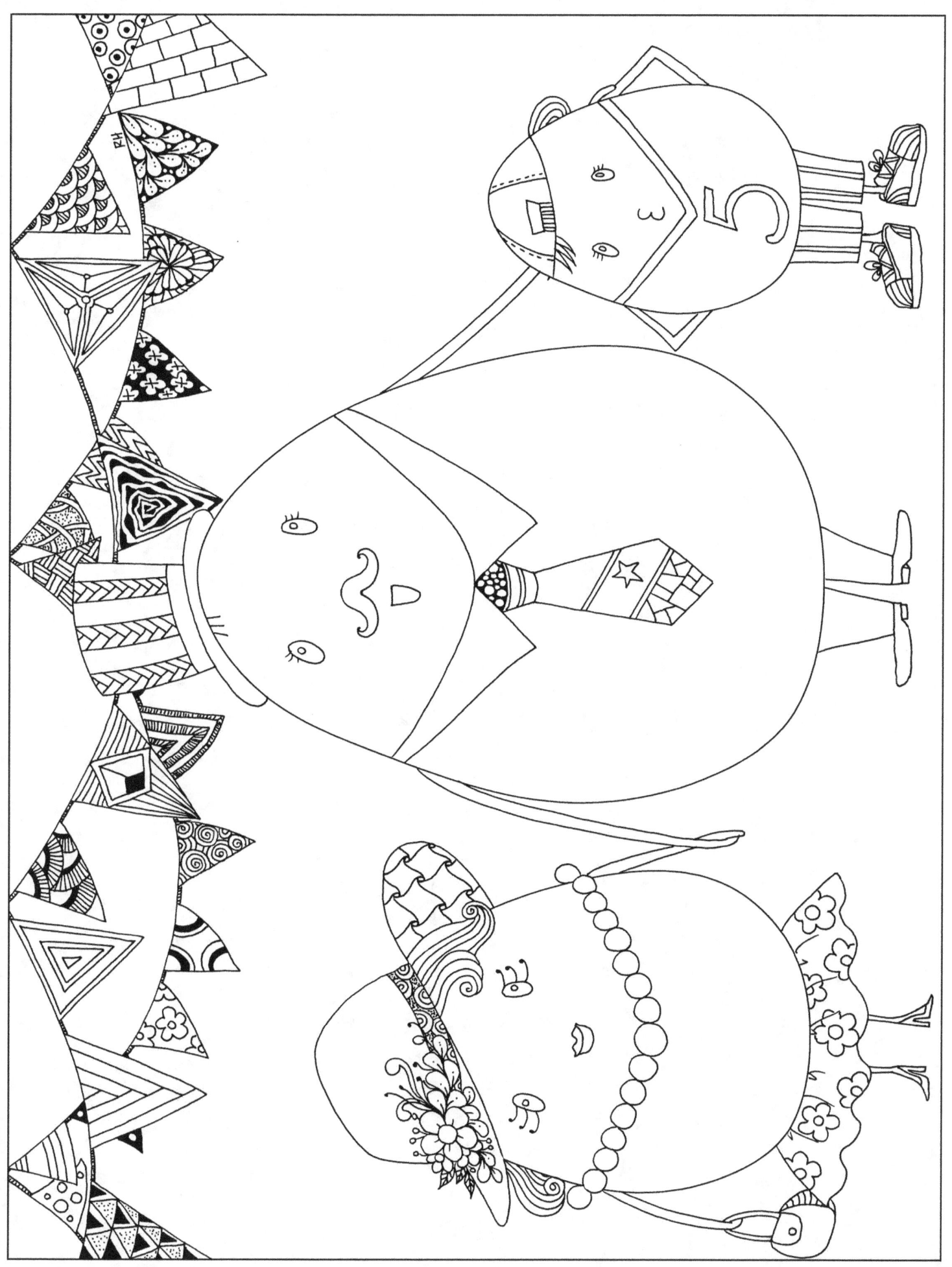

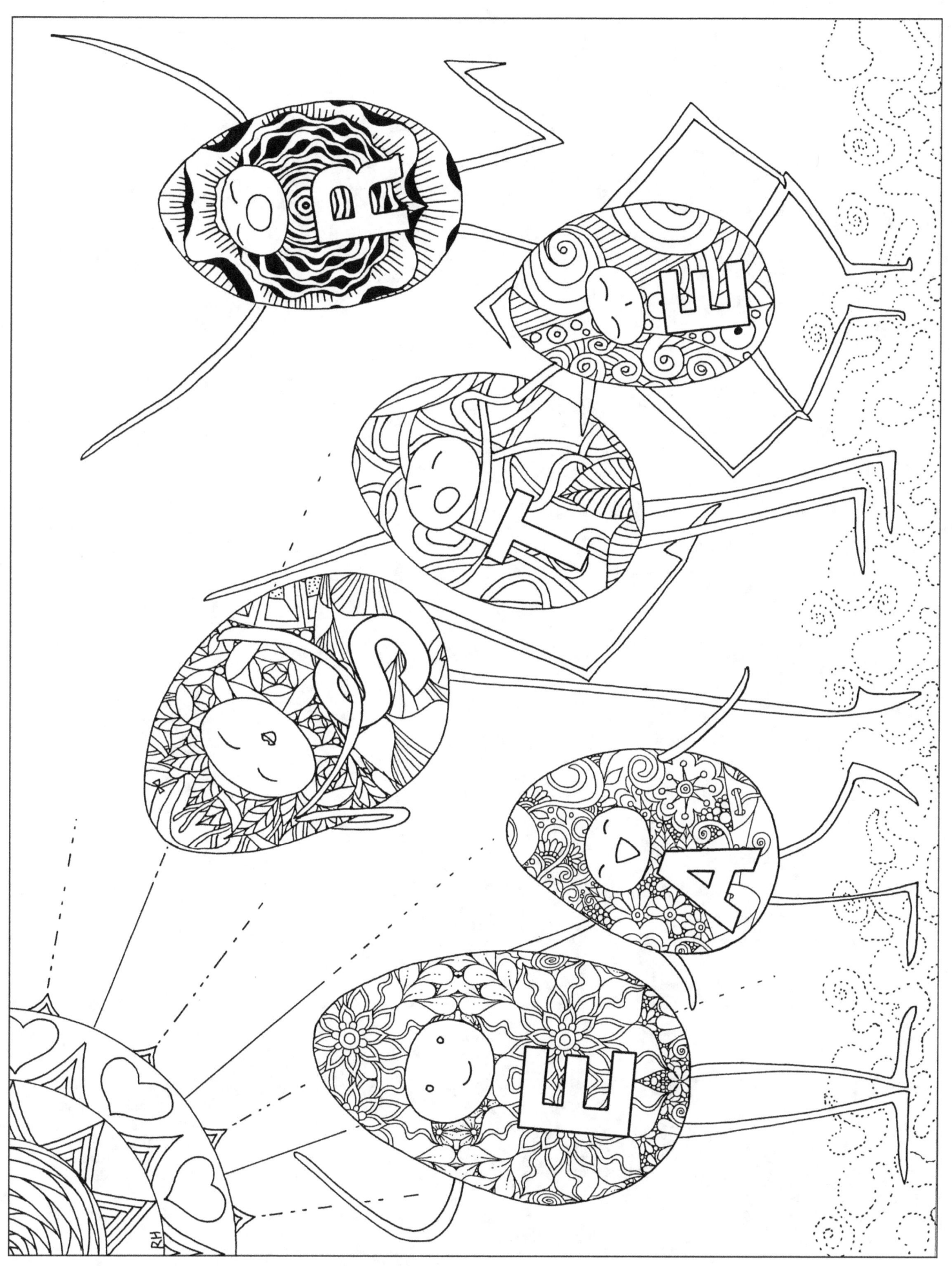

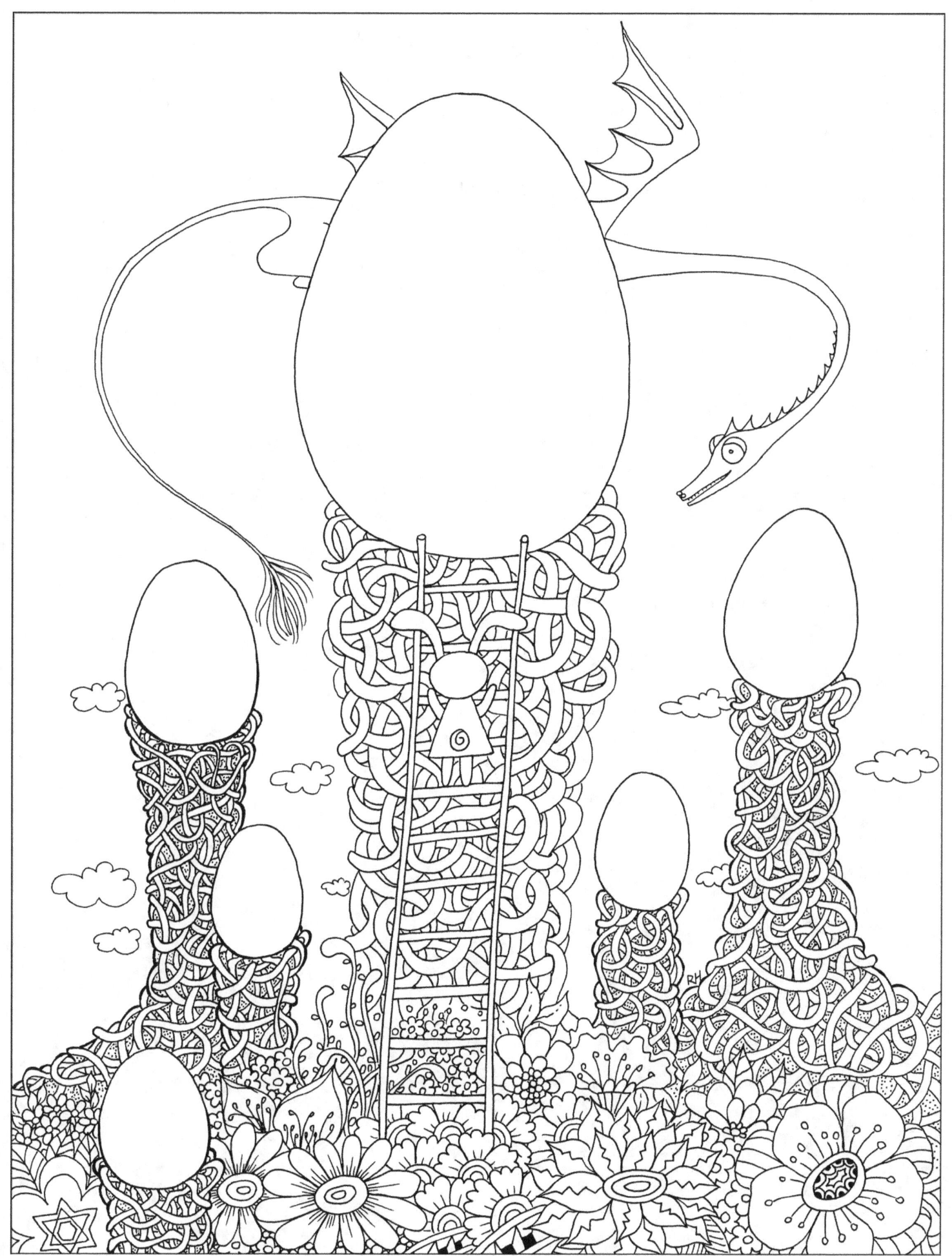

Contributing Artist
Maria Wedel
Denmark

Facebook : AMVWART

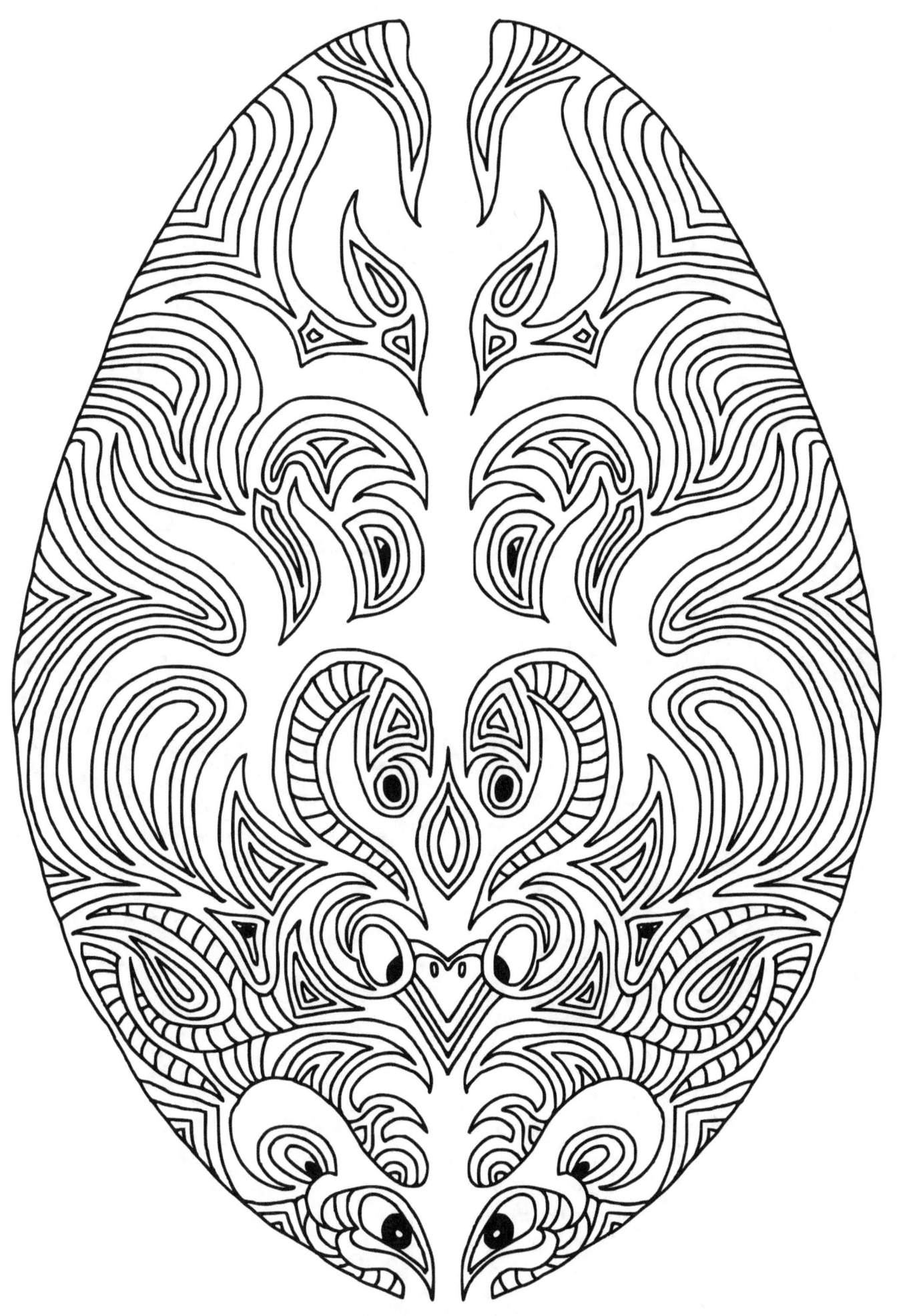

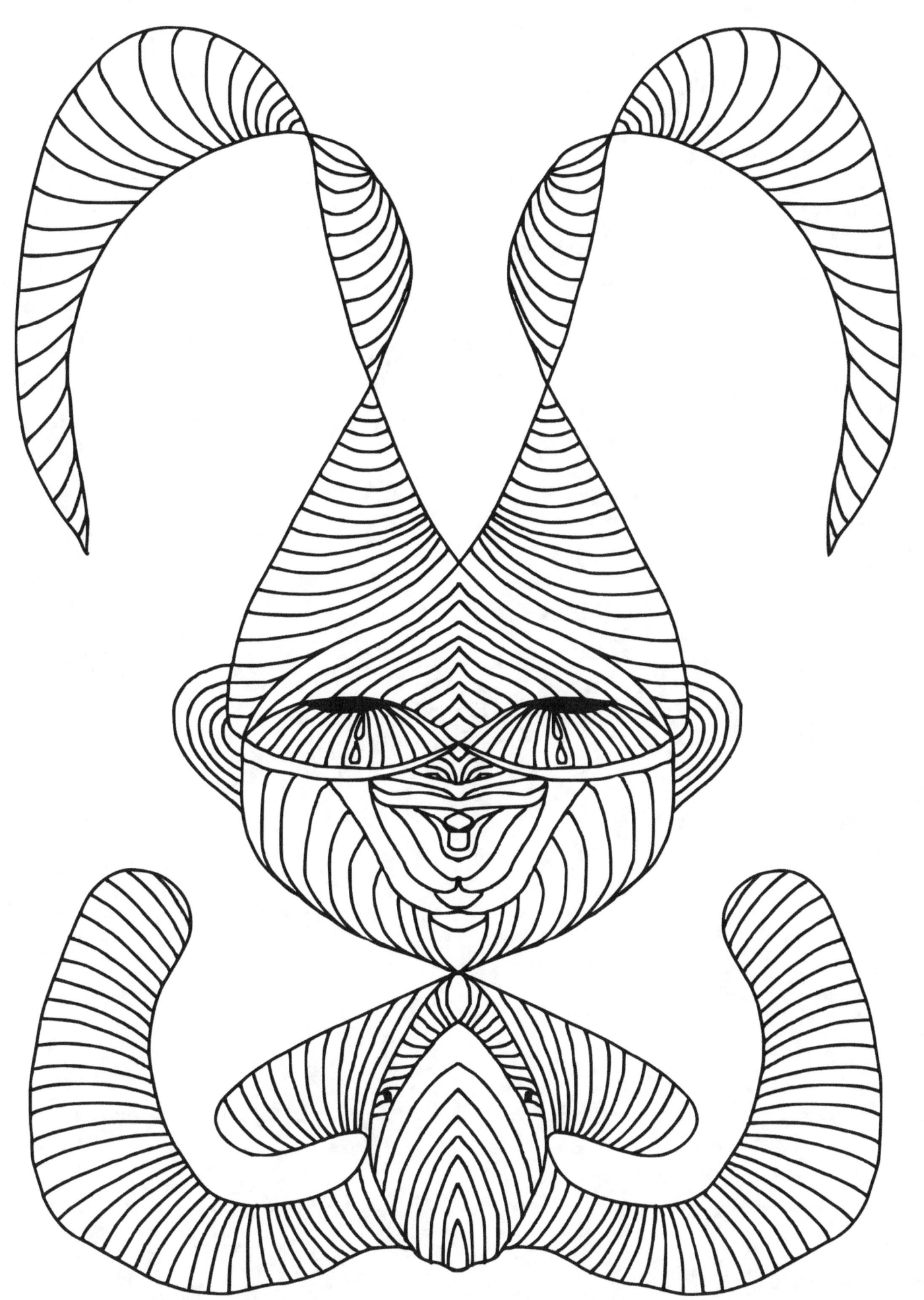

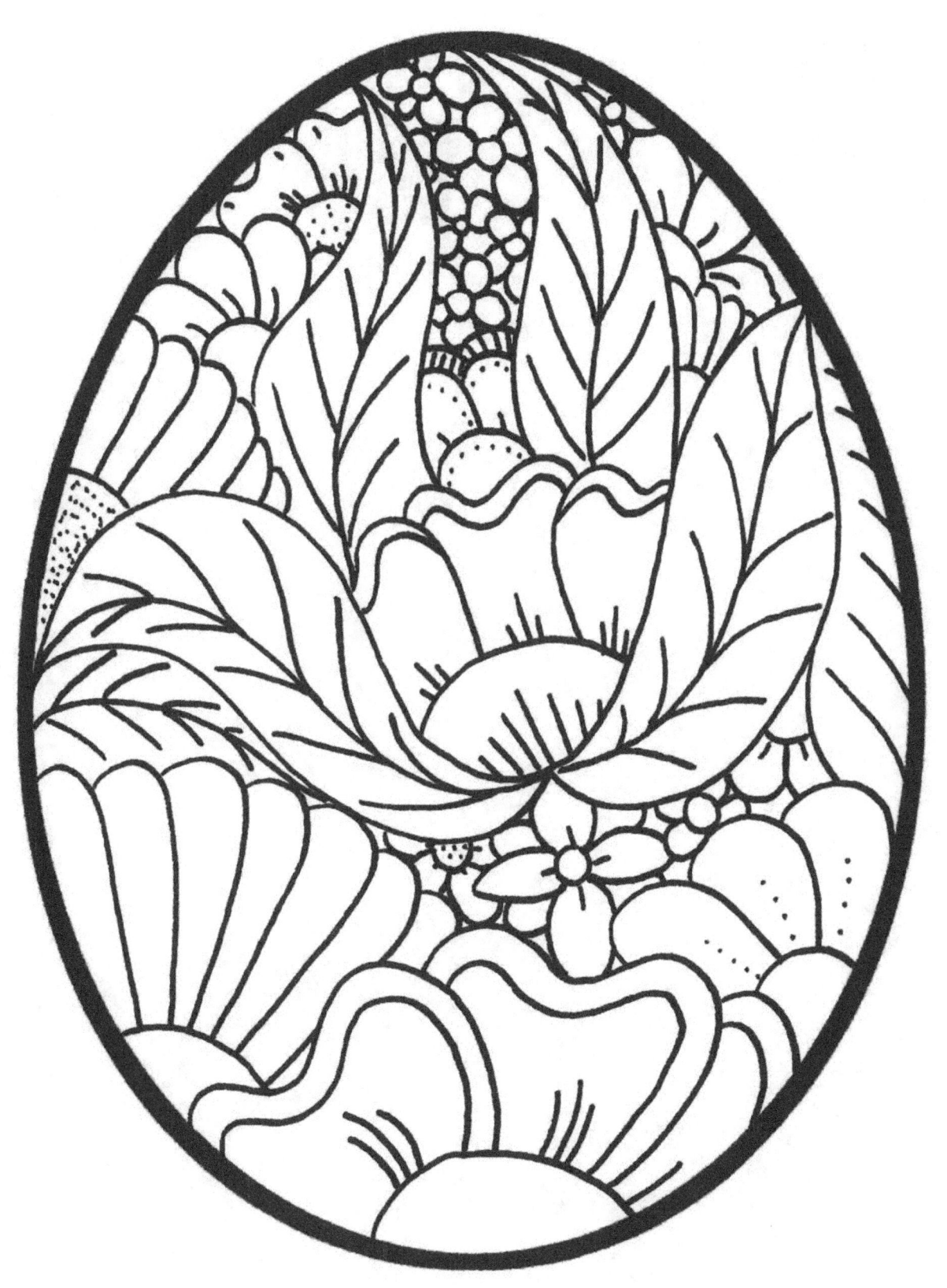

Maria Wedel

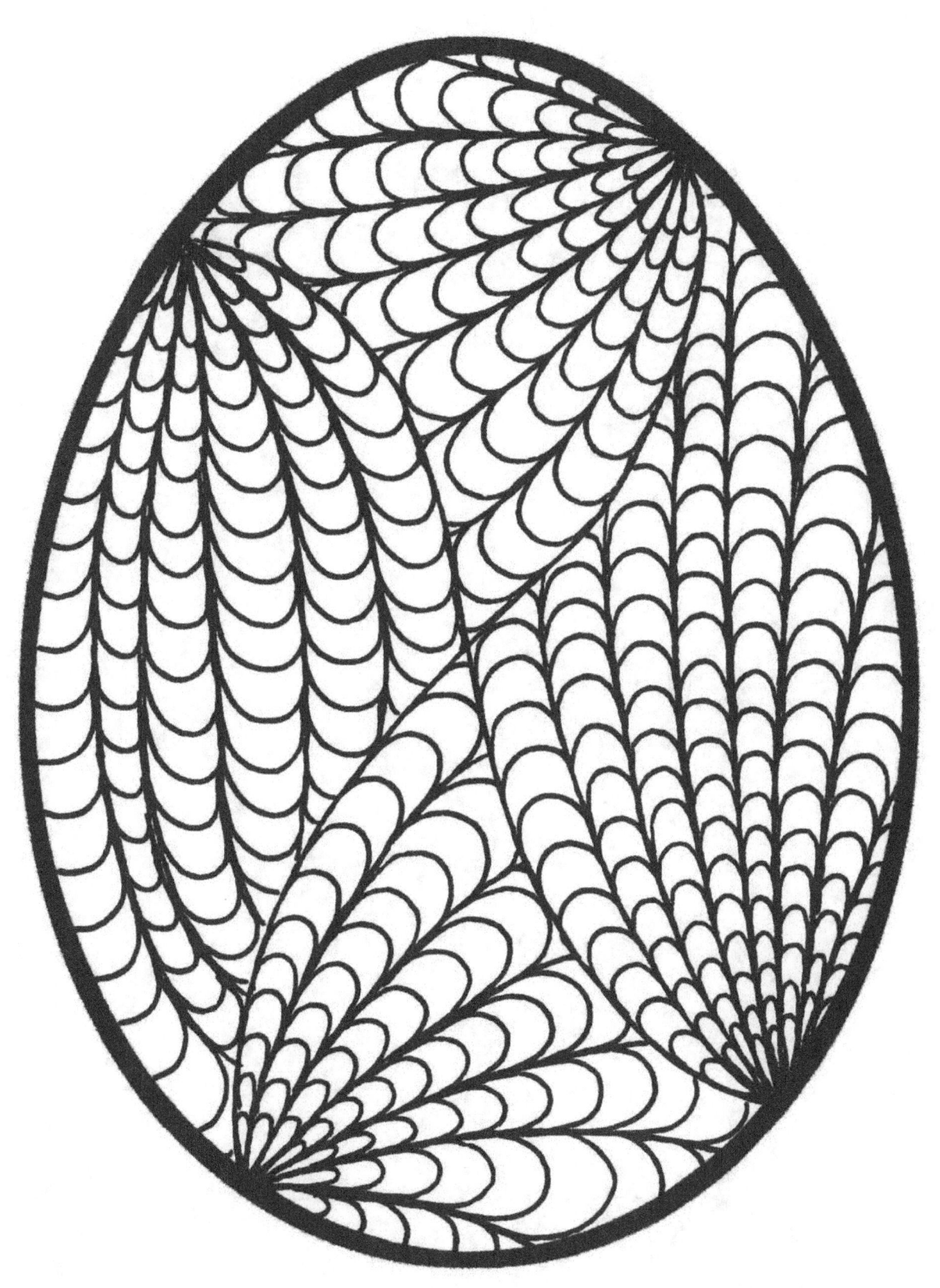

Maria Wedel

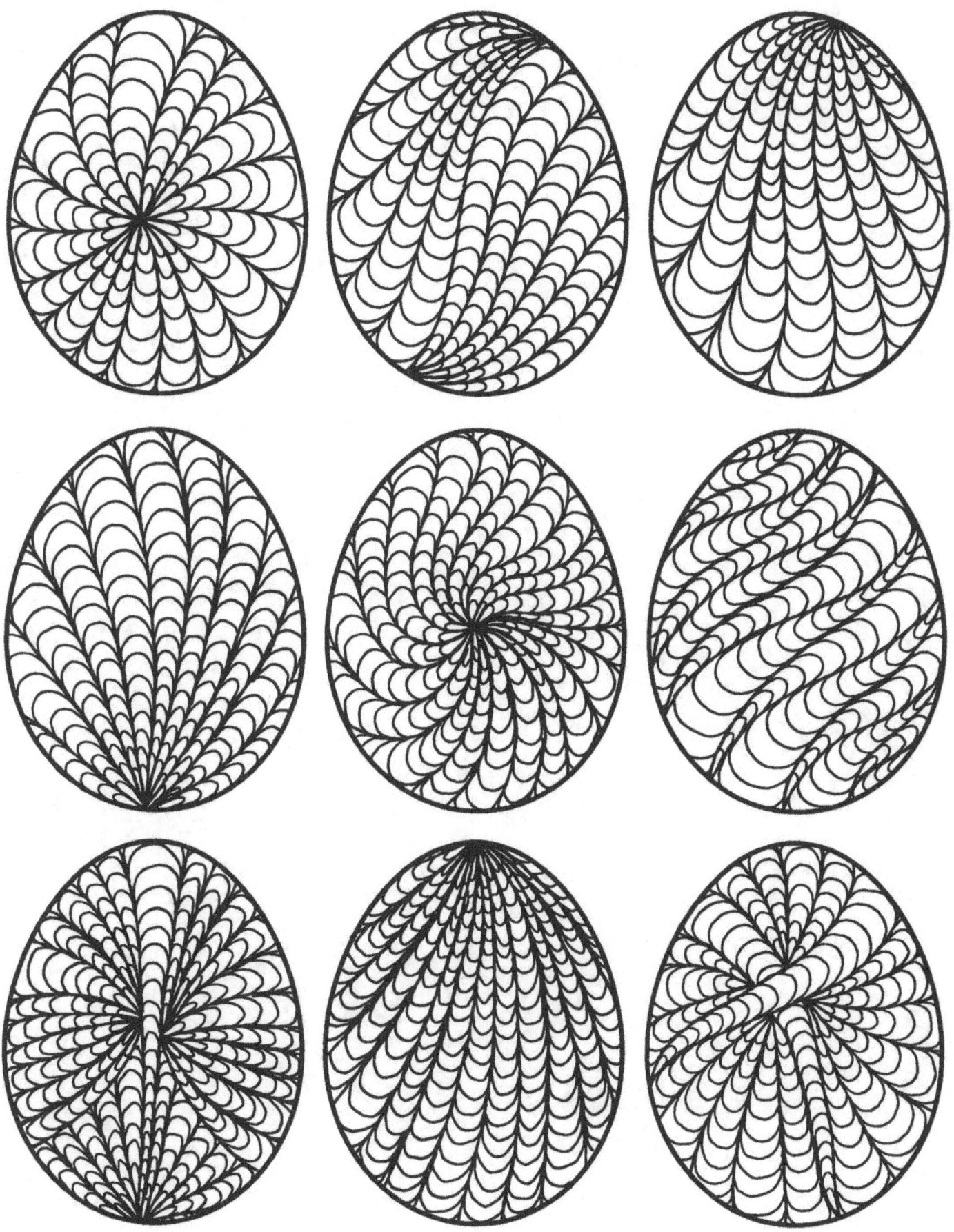

Test your colors here on the samples from
"My Pocket Coloring Companion"
&
"My Coloring Companion"

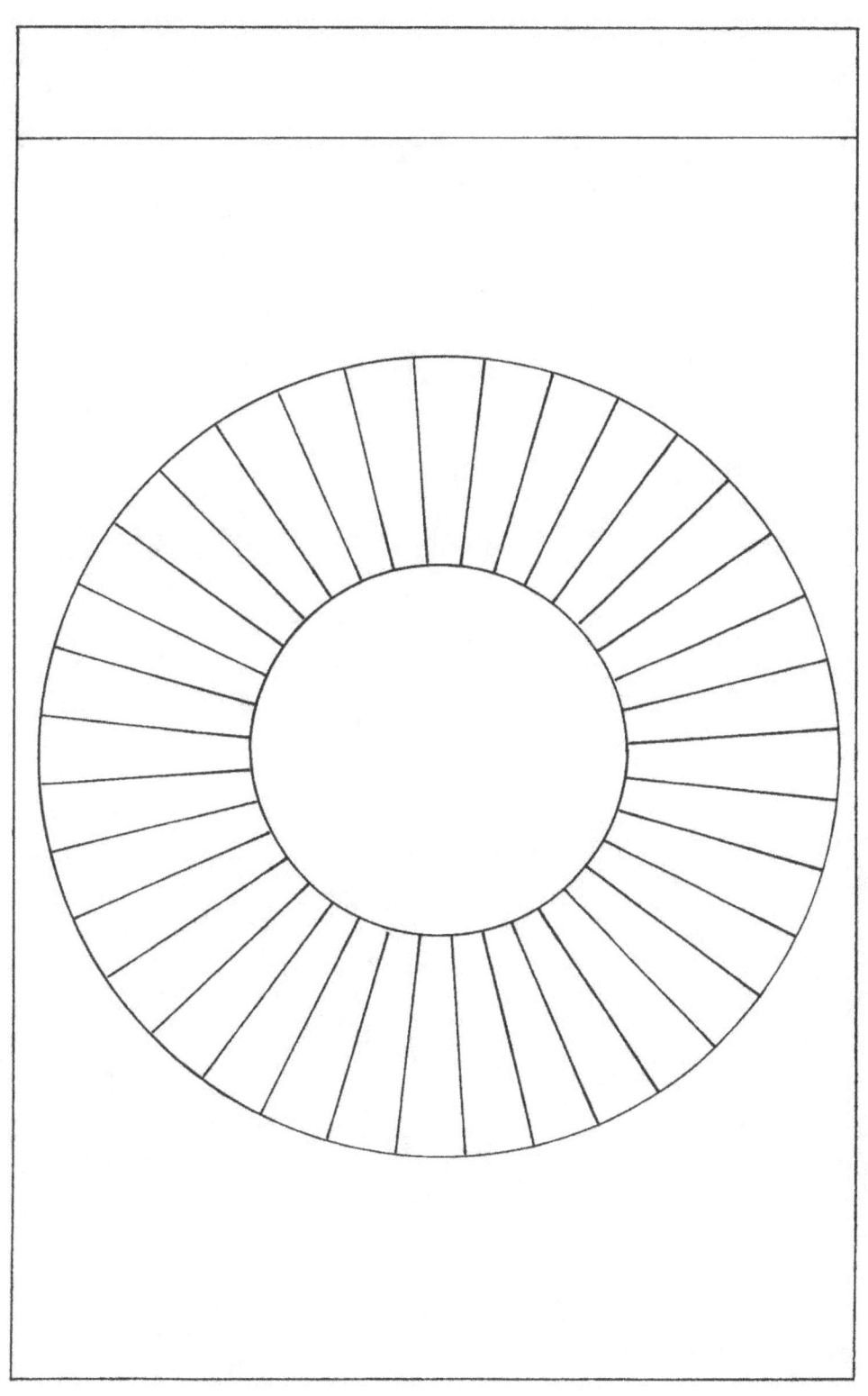

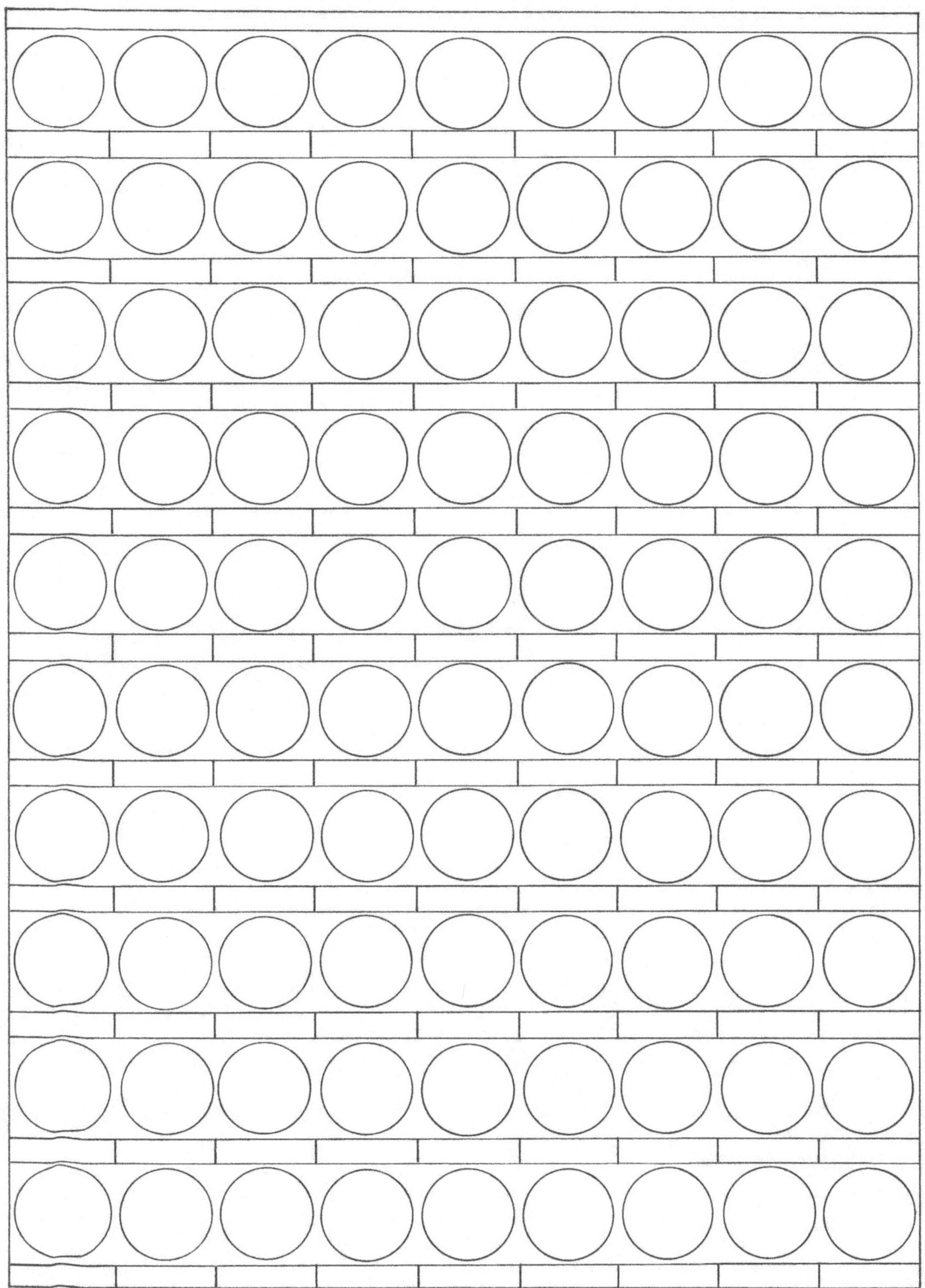

www.ingramcontent.com/pod-product-compliance
Lightning Source LLC
Chambersburg PA
CBHW082341220526
45470CB00008B/2592